Pippa's
ORGANIC
KITCHEN
GARDEN

Pippa's ORGANIC KITCHEN GARDEN

PIPPA GREENWOOD

DORLING KINDERSLEY
London • New York • Sydney
www.dk.com

A DORLING KINDERSLEY BOOK
www.dk.com

*To everyone who, like me, loves home-grown fruit and vegetables,
and to all those who helped to make the Gardeners' World
filming and the writing of this book such fun.*

PROJECT EDITOR Pamela Brown
ART EDITORS Janet James, Ursula Dawson

SENIOR MANAGING EDITOR Mary-Clare Jerram
MANAGING ART EDITOR Lee Griffiths

PICTURE RESEARCH Anna Grapes
SPECIAL PHOTOGRAPHY Peter Anderson
DTP DESIGNER Louise Paddick
PRODUCTION MANAGER Julian Deeming

First published in Great Britain in 1999
by Dorling Kindersley Limited,
9 Henrietta Street, London WC2E 8PS

A CIP catalogue for this book is available from the British Library.
ISBN 0 7513 08056

Reproduced by Colourscan, Singapore
Printed and bound in Italy

CONTENTS

MAKING & RUNNING THE PLOT

MAKING & RUNNING THE PLOT

The decision to create a kitchen garden, both for my own use and for BBC television's Gardeners' World, was finally made only a couple of months before the series went on air. It was a real rush getting the fences up and the paths laid before the camera crew arrived for the first day's filming, but it has been tremendous fun and we have produced some splendid crops. I always try to keep pesticides to a minimum whatever I am growing, but when it comes to fruit and vegetables, I will not use chemicals at all. Knowing there are millions of others who feel the same, it was important that this kitchen garden should be organic. The sense of satisfaction you get from harvesting (and better still, eating) your own freshly picked, home-grown, pesticide-free food takes some beating. You need not be an experienced gardener to achieve it, so do get out there and have a go.

Pippa Greenwood

PIPPA'S OWN PLOT

After six months, the kitchen garden looked very much as it does here and just how I dreamt it would be. The greenhouse has still to be built, and the fruit trees need time to mature, but by midsummer I had picked my first strawberries, and we were on our way.

WIGWAMS OF BEANS

Top corner bed

This bed contains the brassicas – *calabrese*, *sprouting broccoli*, *cauliflowers*, and *swedes*. *Sweet corn* needs to be grown in a block for good pollination; the row of *Jerusalem artichokes* by the gate will provide a useful winter feast.

EXPECTED YIELD

Yields vary greatly with growing conditions and varieties chosen. These figures give an approximate guide.

VEGETABLE OR FRUIT	YIELD
Carrots	5kg (11lb 4oz) per 3m (10ft) row
Courgettes	15 courgettes per plant
French beans	3kg (7lb) per 3m (10ft) row
Peas	3.5–4.5kg (8–10lb) per 3m (10ft) row
Potatoes (early)	1.5kg (3lb 6oz) per plant
Runner beans	1kg (2lb 4oz) per plant
Spinach	3kg (7lb) per 3m (10ft) row
Strawberries	750g (1lb 8oz) per plant
Sweet corn	2 cobs per plant
Tomatoes	1.75kg (4lb) per outdoor plant

Bottom corner bed

Much of this bed was put down to *potatoes*, whose roots help to break up heavy ground. *Cordon tomatoes* and bright-stemmed *chard* fill the remaining space.

ONIONS DRYING IN SUN

The greenhouse
This is a future project. It will be used for starting off crops such as *sweet corn*, *courgettes*, and *tomatoes*, and will be invaluable for growing tender *peppers*, *melons*, and *aubergines*. The frames will have many uses, including hardening off seedlings, growing plants on, and protecting winter crops such as *lettuce*.

COMPOST BINS

— RHUBARB FORCER

— HERBS IN POTS

Bottom centre bed
Leeks, *garlic*, and *onions* are combined with *carrots* and *parsnips* to combat two pests in one go. The onion smell should deter carrot fly, and the aroma of carrots, the onion fly.

Top centre and end beds
Rhubarb and *globe artichokes* grow together in the end triangular bed, with some lettuce in between. The top centre bed contains *beans* and *peas*, *courgettes* and *marrows*, and several varieties of *tomato*.

Fruit patch
The *fruit trees* will take a while to get going and produce fruit, as will the *raspberries* and *blackberry*. But the *stawberries* yielded a mouthwatering crop, and in the gaps I managed to fit in a couple of *courgette* plants.

GETTING STARTED

Transforming a sloping patch of rough grassland into a kitchen garden was the start of a whole new adventure. I had to get back to basics and plan a layout suited to the plot's shape, as well as choose the best fruit and vegetables for the site and soil.

YOU MAY HAVE LITTLE CHOICE over where you site your fruit and vegetables if space is limited or your garden is already established. But if options are still open, or you can rearrange existing features, the right site can make a world of difference to how well your plants grow and crop.

Finding the best site

Most fruit and vegetables need plenty of sunshine if they are to thrive and a gentle slope that catches the sun for most of the day is an advantage since the soil will warm up faster in spring. A windy site is not ideal. My hillside plot, although sunny, can be rather windswept, but I am counting on the fact that the weather is at its windiest when there are fewest crops growing. Moreover, good air circulation helps to decrease humidity and so reduces problems with many fungal diseases, which thrive in damp conditions. Wind-pollinated crops such as sweet corn

should also do better. But where wind becomes counter-productive, you will need to erect or plant a suitable windbreak (*see p.14*).

Frost is almost impossible to avoid completely, but make sure you don't plant fruit in a frost pocket, since damaged blossom will result in a poor or non-existent harvest. You will no doubt have to compromise over how you fit some things in, but try to site vegetables within your plot where growing conditions suit them best. Avoid a fast-draining spot like the top of a slope for thirsty plants such as courgettes, and if one corner is a little damp and shady, use it for rocket or lettuce. Fruit trees and long-term crops, such as globe artichokes and rhubarb, need careful positioning at the outset. I decided to grow my fruit in one large area and put perennial vegetables in a separate, smaller bed (*see p.9*).

On the whole, vegetables prefer a neutral to slightly alkaline soil, while fruits tend to like it neutral to slightly acid, so it makes sense to check your soil pH (*see p.19*). Bear this in mind when choosing what to grow and where, and also before deciding what soil preparation is needed.

Organic values

I really do care about what I eat and there was no doubt that this garden was to be organic. Although I had grown a few crops since moving here, I was still spending a lot of time and money sourcing organically grown fruit and vegetables. It is possible to take organic gardening to varying degrees. With just a little extra thought and planning it is fairly easy

In the beginning
Transforming uncultivated ground like this into a kitchen garden makes starting most other vegetable patches seem simple, yet in four months strawberries and calabrese were ready to harvest.

to eliminate chemicals, and, if you do not have the time or space, it is not essential to make your own fertilizer from a patch of comfrey or grow and dig in green manures. You will certainly need to look after the soil well and nourish it, choose disease-resistant varieties, and use pest barriers, but I am convinced that the small amount of effort required to produce fresh, chemical-free food is more than worth it.

Choosing tools

However small your garden, it is essential to get yourself some basic tools. It is all very well struggling along with a spade with a wobbly handle and a trowel that came as a free gift, but it will make every job take longer and seem more of a task than a pleasure. So whether you treat yourself or persuade friends and family to buy you what you really need for your next birthday, I recommend that you arm yourself with some decent-quality equipment. I reckon that the bare essentials are: a spade (with a tread on the top of the blade for good grip), a fork, a

trowel, a rake (for soil and seedbed preparation), secateurs, a hoe (for weeding and marking out seed drills), a garden line (to achieve straight rows), a watering can, a hosepipe (if your kitchen garden is not close to an outdoor tap or other water source), a dibber (for pricking out and transplanting), and perhaps a multi-pronged cultivator (for weeding and breaking up medium-sized clods of soil when preparing the ground for sowing or planting).

Always hold tools before you buy, checking that they are comfortable to use and of a suitable size and weight. My tools have been acquired over a number of years and include several excellent secondhand ones picked up at local auctions. Old spades and hoes can be sharpened to an extremely efficient cutting edge, and often prove that the best tools are not necessarily the newest and shiniest.

PLANNING WHAT TO GROW

Deciding how to fill the plot is great fun. For me, browsing through seed catalogues is the ultimate form of window-shopping. It gives a chance to compare the attractions of new introductions with familiar, tried-and-tested varieties.

THE AMOUNT OF SPACE you have and how much time you can devote to gardening are key factors. But even more important, choose to grow the things you actually want to eat. It is no use getting carried away by the good looks of ruby chard or the trendiness of rocket if these are not vegetables you enjoy. My choice has been governed by what I know the family likes. As time goes on, I will no doubt make some changes and introduce new vegetables, but in the first year I have avoided most brassicas and less-than-favourite fruits such as gooseberries. For the moment, we prefer to feast on tomatoes, potatoes, raspberries, and freshly picked sweet corn.

Which variety?

Sending off for lots of seed catalogues gives you a useful source of information about the varieties available and allows you to shop at leisure. Taste and texture are one of my main reasons for growing my own vegetables, although pretty well whatever you grow will be an improvement on the shop-bought version. Catalogue and seed-packet descriptions can help you choose. Some varieties – 'Gardener's Delight' or 'Marmande' tomatoes (*above picture*), for instance – are renowned for their flavour. However, if you are still unsure, try growing several varieties of the same vegetable, making sure that between them they will crop over as long a period as possible; you can often extend the cropping period by weeks or sometimes months. If stored in a cool, dry, dark place, most seeds will keep for a couple of years, sometimes more, without germination rates being

significantly reduced, so you can always use the remains of a packet another season. Most seed companies now clearly state which varieties show resistance to common pests and diseases, something organic gardeners should definitely note.

Use space efficiently

To make the most of every scrap of space when drawing up your plan of what to grow where, try intercropping. This may sound complicated, but nothing could be simpler. All it means is that you

Undercropping to maximise space
Like intercropping, this makes use of the gaps between vegetables. Lettuce, spinach, and chards can be grown among tall plants such as sweet corn without affecting the quality of the crops.

Fruit tree shapes
Trained cordons and espaliers take up a minimum of space, and a bush tree, although slightly smaller than a half-standard, will yield good crops.

CORDON   ESPALIER   BUSH

sow or plant a fast-growing, fast-maturing crop, such as lettuce, between a slow-growing, slow-maturing crop, such as parsnips. The first crop will be harvested long before the slower-growing one needs the space to itself. I even raised an early crop of lettuce in between a row of extra-early potatoes under a mini-polytunnel.

Make successional sowings, where possible, to ensure a continuous supply of vegetables such as carrots and lettuce. Together with a carefully planned choice of varieties, this will help to minimize the common problem of gluts followed by famines.

Principles of rotation

However small your vegetable garden, you should try to incorporate a rotation system, because by growing groups of vegetables on a different part of the plot each year, they will be less likely to succumb to soil-borne pests and diseases. It will also help to maintain the necessary balance of nutrients in the soil. If your garden is very small, you can still make sure that you grow each vegetable on a different spot every year, ideally leaving a gap of two or three years before your root crops, say, return to the place where you first grew them.

To a certain extent you can choose what goes where, but there are a few principles you should follow. Try to group crops so that all your brassicas are together. Tomatoes and potatoes should either be in the same bed or, if in separate beds, do not let them follow each other in the rotation plan. Carrots, celery, parsley, and parsnips should be kept together, as should onions, garlic, shallots, and leeks. The legumes (peas and beans) should also be grown in the same bed. Most rotation plans put carrots and parsnips in a separate bed from onions and their relatives, but I have grown them together for the good reason that both groups of plants have strongly aromatic foliage, and the smell of carrots and parsnips should help to deter onion fly while that of onions, leeks, and garlic will deter carrot fly.

Selecting fruit

When choosing fruit, remember that it does take up quite a lot of space, so you should always check the label carefully to ensure you can give any plant sufficient room. You will also need to check that you have selected varieties that are self-fertile or are capable of pollinating each other (that is, they are in flower at the same time), or you may end up with an extremely disappointing crop. Catalogues usually contain pollination details, and a specialist supplier will be able to advise you.

Locally-bought plants should be well suited to prevailing conditions, but a specialist grower, regardless of where they are based, will be able to recommend the best varieties for your part of the country. They will also be able to advise on the most suitable rootstock for both tree shape and site. Fitting fruit trees into a garden is difficult when space is limited. I have planted bush trees (*see above*), but espaliers, fans, and cordons, take up less room and can be trained against walls or fences.

Taste and texture are particularly important, as fruit represents a long-term investment and trees may not crop for the first few years. Again, it's worth reading catalogues and books, but nothing beats trying the varieties yourself. Look out for tasting days at nurseries and gardens, and sample as many kinds as you can before making your selection.

SITE PREPARATION

When starting a kitchen garden, you will need to consider the various permanent features that may be needed. If carefully planned and well constructed, paths, fences, and even the supports for soft fruit can prove long-lasting assets.

MY OWN PLOT IS probably larger than most, but even in small gardens, you will need to consider how to arrange the space, what size to make individual beds, and how to provide access to them and perhaps to the whole area. I decided to divide my kitchen garden into six beds (*see pp.8–9*): four oblong vegetable beds for easy rotation, each measuring about 3.6m (12ft) by 4.8m (16ft), one large bed for permanent fruit, and one small triangle for the "miscellaneous extras", perennial vegetables such as rhubarb and globe artichokes.

Access & protection

Main, frequently used paths need to be of sturdy construction and easy and safe to use in all weathers. I decided to make those in this garden of compacted scalpings (rock chippings in a gradation of sizes) with a red brick edging. This gives a surface that weathers well and blends in with the landscape. Paths entirely of brick pavers look good, too, but are more expensive and are inclined to become slippery in winter. The width of paths is important. Where space permits, make them broad enough so you can park a wheelbarrow and walk past it with ease. My own beds are too large for me to reach every part while standing on the paths, so I use wooden planks as movable paths – a good way to avoid unnecessarily damaging the soil while minimizing the amount of productive land that is lost.

Our area is home to huge populations of rabbits, so rabbit-proof fencing was essential. Two sides of my plot have been rabbit-proofed for several years,

Rabbit-proofing
As long as it is securely fastened to posts or an existing fence, and buried in the soil to prevent tunnelling underneath, chicken wire should keep rabbits out.

one alongside the goose run and another along the boundary fence. The other two are bounded by attractive split-chestnut hurdles to which I have attached rabbit-proof wire netting. To keep rabbits out, this needs to have a 2.5cm (1in) mesh and be 1.2–1.4m (4–4½ft) high. The bottom 30cm (12in) should be buried underground, angled outwards to make it more difficult for rabbits to tunnel underneath. If you are not attaching netting to existing fencing, it can be supported by 7.5–10cm (3–4in) diameter pressure-treated posts and taut horizontal strands of galvanized wire.

In a windswept site you will probably need to plant or put up windbreaks. I have chosen hedges of native trees – hawthorn, blackthorn, dog rose, and guelder rose. The small plants sold for hedging take a while to get going, but then, after a year or two, start to grow quickly to the required height. Hedges make a good windbreak because they filter the wind, as do hazel or willow hurdles. If fencing is to provide shelter, it is best if the laths form an open construction, preferably to filter the wind by about 50 per cent. A closely boarded fence can easily blow down in strong gusts.

If you decide to devote an area to soft fruit, it is wise to put up some sort of fruit cage to protect against marauding birds. You can buy ready-made cages, which generally consist of an aluminium frame and netting, or construct one yourself using timber or metal posts. To protect individual or small numbers of plants, stick canes or stakes in the ground, put an upturned flowerpot on top of each and drape over some fruit-cage netting. Secure the netting firmly at ground level. Raspberries need a permanent support system. I have used sturdy pressure-treated timber posts driven firmly into the ground, to which I attached horizontal galvanized wires to support the canes (*see p.84*).

It is likely that you will have to do quite a lot of this sort of construction work during the winter, but do try not to damage the soil in the process, by trampling on it while it is wet.

Essential recycling

In any kind of garden a compost heap is a real boon, but in an organic kitchen garden it is a necessity, so plan in a space for it at the start. In a sunny site, the heap will warm up and produce compost more quickly. Whether you buy a ready-made bin, a kit, or decide to construct your own container depends on available space, time, and money. I have chosen a traditional wooden double-bin that came in kit form, and a couple designed to look like beehives. You

Compost with style
Designed to look like beehives, these compost bins would be ideal in a garden where every component needs to look as attractive as possible. Two bins will give a continuous supply of compost.

may have space for one compost bin only, but if you can fit it in, a double-bin or two-berth system is best (or two bins side by side). This allows you to be filling and making compost in one bin while emptying the other. It is essential that softwood timber is pressure treated with preservative to delay rotting and that the bin's size and position allows you to inspect, turn, and empty the compost easily.

A water butt is also extremely useful, although to be of significant help it needs to be attached to the downpipe leading from a roof or other collection surface. Alternatively, you can attach a butt to the downpipe from a bathroom (recycled bath water should not cause any damage to your crops). A water diverter makes this a simple task. These are readily available from DIY stores and can be fitted to both square or round plastic downpipes.

PIPPA'S ORGANIC TIPS

■ Adding organic matter to the soil season after season will gradually raise the level of the ground. Allow for this when laying permanent paths.

■ If the vegetable plot is not next to the house, remember that shed, garage, and greenhouse roofs can all be used to collect and channel rainwater into a water butt.

■ A compost heap is indispensable. Choose a double-bin wherever possible and site it so that access is easy and you can reach to turn the compost inside.

CLEARING THE WEEDS

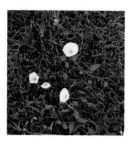

Television viewers were able to see my kitchen garden at its very start, when it was still a weed-ridden field. Not surprisingly, I am the first to recognize that there are two types of weeding – site clearance and day-to-day maintenance.

IT IS OFTEN SAID that a weed is "any plant growing where you don't want it". When I started out, my plot was edge-to-edge unwanted inhabitants. Because we began work on the garden during the winter, even if I had been prepared to use them, weedkillers were not an option.

Working methods

Used at the wrong time of year, while plant growth is slow or virtually non-existent, glyphosate, the systemic weedkiller best suited to clearing land of perennial weeds, has little effect. If you are willing to make a concession to your organic principles and use chemicals, there are several proprietary brands based on glyphosate. If applied according to the instructions on the packet, these work well, clearing most weeds in one application in my experience, and killing even the more pernicious kinds such as docks and nettles after a second application. If you want to avoid chemicals but have plenty of preparation time, covering the ground with old carpet, black polythene, or similar light-excluding material will gradually smother them, but it will take a year or more to deal with the most troublesome.

Hand clearance, by forking and digging, can produce good results but it is very time-consuming and requires a phenomenal amount of energy. Whatever you do, if soil is infested with weeds such as bindweed (*above picture*), couch grass, and dock, do not be tempted to use a powered cultivator since this will chop them up, making the problem worse in the long run. When forking and digging, it is essential

to avoid slicing the tap roots of dock and dandelion, or long, underground shoots or roots of ground elder and bindweed, since these can regenerate from even the tiniest section. Remove whole roots or as many pieces as you can, or you might find that one weed root has sprouted into at least four more plants.

If you are clearing rough ground like mine during winter, there will be plenty of weeds without any foliage. It is best to assume that all root material you come across needs removing, so that you have a blank canvas at the start, although a few weeds are likely to be a problem for several years, however thorough your weeding. Some species are much more prevalent than others on certain types of soil, but those shown opposite generally cause the biggest headache in fruit and vegetable plots.

Look to the future

Weed seeds are notoriously long-lived and may remain dormant in the soil for years, germinating over a period, so regular hoeing or hand-weeding will still be needed in future seasons. Mulching should help to suppress and smother weeds and, since on damp soil it also helps to conserve moisture, it is of double benefit (*see p.28*).

Whatever method you use to remove weeds, you should compost only those that you know could not possibly survive the process. I never compost anything with pernicious roots or shoots or any weed that has set seed, or indeed looks as if it is about to do so. It is not worth the risk. Instead, put these weeds straight into the bin or onto the bonfire.

THE USUAL TROUBLE-MAKERS

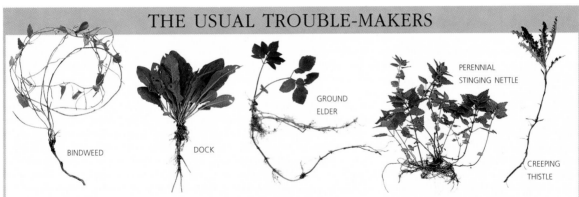

BINDWEED

DOCK

GROUND ELDER

PERENNIAL STINGING NETTLE

CREEPING THISTLE

Annual meadow grass

An easy annual weed to pull out, but try to catch it before it sets seed and rapidly multiplies. It often spreads into vegetable beds from nearby grassed areas.

Bindweed

A perennial that starts to shoot above ground in late spring and early summer, its pink or white flowers appearing in late summer (*see facing page, top*). If clearing land or digging in winter, watch for its long, white, fleshy roots in the soil and try to remove all fragments. Any that remain will produce new plants.

Common chickweed

An annual but persistent because it grows and sets seed through autumn and winter. It forms small-leaved clumps with tiny, starry white flowers. Hand-weed or hoe if off.

Couch grass

A perennial that spreads by forming a network of underground shoots and also by seed. Dig out these shoots, trying not to slice them; pieces left in the ground will readily resprout. If it appears among

growing crops, remove the flowerheads before they have a chance to set seed.

Creeping buttercup

A perennial that spreads by runners, so that the rosettes of leaves quickly form a chain of plants. It also self-seeds. Although reasonably easy to uproot, it can be very invasive. Yellow buttercup flowers appear in summer.

Creeping thistle

The long roots are difficult to dig out entirely, and the prickly rosettes of leaves are likely to reappear for several seasons after clearing new ground. A pernicious perennial – repeated efforts are usually necessary.

Dandelion

Familiar perennial whose tap roots need to be removed completely or they will reshoot. A long narrow tool, or even an old kitchen knife, is useful for removing them. Try not to let flowers set seed.

Dock

Perennial with similar tap roots to a dandelion's and needing the same

treatment. If possible, pull docks out while still small, and don't let them flower and shed their prolific seed.

Ground elder

A pernicious perennial that needs to be cleared from any site destined for fruit or vegetables. Its network of long, fleshy, underground shoots is difficult to disentangle from the roots of other plants. The shoots snap easily and form new plants. Try to dig out every piece.

Hairy bittercress

Small annual that sets seed with alarming speed. It can be kept under control with frequent hoeing or hand-weeding. Mulching helps, too.

Groundsel

An annual that can be kept at bay by hoeing. Alternatively hand-weed before it flowers and sets seed.

Shepherd's purse

Like other annuals, this is likely to be more of a problem once the kitchen garden is under way. It self-seeds rapidly. Hoe or hand-weed.

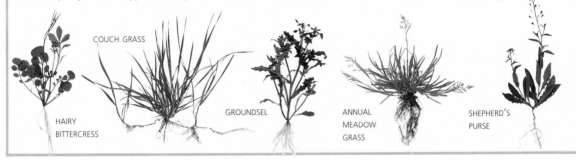

HAIRY BITTERCRESS

COUCH GRASS

GROUNDSEL

ANNUAL MEADOW GRASS

SHEPHERD'S PURSE

SOIL ESSENTIALS

Soil texture and structure, nutrient levels, and acidity or alkalinity vary hugely from garden to garden and can even sometimes vary within a garden. So, before you set to work improving your soil, investigate its characteristics first.

GROWING VEGETABLES usually makes you all too aware of what kind of soil you have. Heavy clay, like mine, tends to be wet and "claggy", you can mould a handful into a sticky ball. It makes digging hard work, and is slow to warm up in spring, delaying outdoor sowing. You can often make an earlier start on light, sandy soil, but because it drains so freely, it doesn't hold on to nutrients so well. If you rub sandy soil between your fingers, you can sometimes feel the grains. Soil over chalk is similarly free-draining. That much sought-after category of a good loam is the ideal, since it manages to combine adequate drainage with good moisture retention.

Adding organic matter

Whatever type of soil you have, it will benefit from the addition of organic matter. I have incorporated huge quantities of well-rotted manure into my heavy clay. My concerns about BSE mean that I am not prepared to use cow manure, so most of the manure used here has come from a free-range pig farm or local horse stables. If you can get hold of it, pig manure is superb and, provided it is well rotted, does not smell strongly. Stable manure often contains a high proportion of wood chippings or sawdust, which can cause problems by using up nitrogen in the soil to the detriment of growing plants. Check it out before you buy or, if possible, get it from a stables where the horses stand on rubber matting.

Garden compost is another essential in an organic garden. It costs nothing, you can make it on site and, like manure, it will help to enhance both the structure

The finest ingredient
Digging in manure benefits every type of soil. It opens up clay, improving drainage and preventing it from baking hard in summer. On sand or chalk, it helps to conserve moisture and nutrients.

and fertility of the soil. It enables sandy soils to retain moisture and aerates and improves drainage on heavy soils. Compost is simple to make, using a combination of kitchen and garden waste, such as annual weeds (as long as they are not setting seed), grass clippings, stems and outer leaves of vegetables, and even some woody material such as chopped up twigs. The time compost takes to mature varies with the size of the heap, its ingredients, the temperature, and season of the year, but it is usually ready to use in three to five months. In a large bin, compost gets hotter and matures faster, as it does if kept adequately moist. To speed things up, you can use a proprietary organic activator, available from garden centres or by mail order (*see p.93*). Never add pernicious perennial weeds such as bindweed or dandelion, or scraps of meat that may attract vermin.

If you have a good supply of deciduous leaves, these can easily be made into leaf-mould. Although it contains relatively low levels of useful nutrients, it is a splendid soil conditioner. Make a simple bin by driving four or more preservative-treated wooden stakes into the ground and attaching a cage of chicken wire. If kept moist, the leaf-mould should be ready in 18–24 months. In small gardens, make it in a black plastic bin-liner. Fill the bag with leaves, add a litre (2 pints) of water, then use a garden fork to prick a few holes. Fold the top over and stack in an out-of-the-way place until the leaf-mould is ready.

Acid or alkaline?
It is worth testing the soil's pH to check acidity or alkalinity levels, since they can be altered to a certain extent. Some kits also show nutrient levels, which may need raising if crops do not thrive.

Tests & treatments

The acidity of a soil is described as its pH. For just a few pounds, you can buy a small kit that allows you to carry out several pH tests around the garden – the pH can vary within a small area. The kits allow you to determine whether your soil is acid (a number below 7), neutral (7), or alkaline (higher than 7). The pH can be raised or lowered slightly: add sulphur to make soil more acid, and rake in lime to make it more alkaline (*see facing page, top*). A few crops have definite preferences (*see p.38 onwards*). After you have incorporated materials to improve soil, you should check the pH again as it may have altered. If crops are clearly not growing as well as they should, occasionally it is because an essential nutrient is lacking. Some kits include tests for this as well.

Both manure and compost will improve a soil's fertility but you may sometimes need to add fertilizer, for hungry crops, such as broccoli and calabrese, for instance. Most organic gardeners find pelleted chicken manure perfectly acceptable, provided it comes from free-range, organically reared birds. Dried blood, fish, and bone meal is also often recommended although as a vegetarian it is not something I would use. Comfrey is an excellent organic fertilizer. You can make a liquid by crushing the leaves, but you need space for a large patch of plants and it's an exceptionally smelly process. An easier option for most people is to buy ready-made comfrey fertilizer from an organic supplier (*see p.93*).

SOWING OUTSIDE

Once the ground is ready, and weather conditions right, many vegetables can be sown direct outside. Some seeds need a warm start inside (see overleaf) *but peas, beans, spinach, salad crops, and root vegetables are all ideal outdoor candidates.*

RAISING VEGETABLES from seed gives you the widest possible selection of varieties. With some plants, such as beans, courgettes, and lettuce, there is a choice between sowing direct into the ground or into pots or trays indoors. But for those that really do not transplant well – all root vegetables, for example – outdoor sowing is essential. It is also sometimes argued that direct-sown plants establish the best. The seeds can be given a little warmth (*see p.24*) and may need protection from birds and mice (*see pp.32–34*).

Good preparation

It is essential for soil to be well-prepared before sowing direct. Once weeded and dug, it needs levelling and raking. You are aiming to create a fine, crumbly surface, removing lumps and stones with each raking. I use the back of a fork to break up

RAKING TO A FINE TILTH

1 *Lightly firm the soil after it has been dug by gently shuffling across the ground, keeping your feet horizontal.*

2 *Draw the rake across several times, varying the direction, until you have a fine, lump-free surface.*

large clods; repeated raking will then give the texture you need. A "fine tilth" means that seeds will be in close contact with the soil and therefore able to take up the moisture they need to germinate. When sowing large seed, such as peas and beans, you can get away with slightly larger particles.

However tempting it may be to start preparing for sowing early in the season, remember that you will only damage the soil if it is wet and sticky, so wait until it has dried out. With heavy ground like mine, this can be a real problem, but using boards to stand on helps to reduce the risk of compaction. The ideal time depends on what you are sowing, but it is always best to delay if conditions are not right; very wet or cold soil will cause seeds to rot. Covering the ground with polythene, cloches, or fleece before you sow (*see p.24*) is one way of making sure it is warm and dry enough when the season is late.

Ready to sow

Most seed is sown in drills, best marked out with a line to keep them straight. With the line in position, make the drill using the point of a trowel or edge of a hoe. The depth will vary according to what you are sowing so check the details on the seed packet. As a rule, fine seeds are sown more shallowly than larger ones, but, whatever the requirements, the drill must be of even depth or the seedlings will emerge at different times and germination may be reduced. Sow sparsely to reduce competition between the seedlings and also the amount of thinning that will be needed. If seed is very fine, I like to mix it first

MAKING A SEED DRILL

1 *Make a drill using the edge of a hoe, or point of a trowel, and a taut garden line to ensure a straight row.*

2 *Sow seed thinly and as evenly as possible but allow for a few seeds to fail or be eaten by mice or birds.*

3 *Use your hand to press the seed into the base of the drill so that it makes good contact with moist soil.*

4 *Gently draw the soil back over the seed, taking care not to displace it. The row should be evenly covered.*

with several times its volume of horticultural (silver) sand to make it easier to handle. Some seeds, such as parsnips, are notorious for their poor germination so station-sow these (*see p.64*). It is also a good idea to intersow with a small, rapidly-maturing crop if germination is known to be slow (*see p.64*). Peas are usually sown in a wide, flat-bottomed drill. I use a spade to take out the drill, cutting along one edge first and then removing the soil to make the drill 2.5–5cm (1–2in) deep and 25–30cm (10–12in) wide. This gives space for three rows of peas, with the rows 10cm (4in) apart (*see facing page, top*).

After sowing, gently press the seed into contact with the moist soil in the drill base and cover to the required depth. Water the row with a fine rose on the watering can so as not to disturb the seed. You will need to keep the soil moist if the rain does not do the job for you. If birds are a problem, you could try the old but effective method of using cotton tied taut between sticks or twigs. The cotton must be taut or there is a risk that the birds could become entangled. A netting tunnel works well (*see p.33*), or humming lines or old audio-cassette tape tied tightly between stakes may act as a deterrent.

Thinning out seedlings is usually best done in stages, over a period, so that you do not over-thin and find yourself left with insufficient plants. You can pull out seedlings root and all or nip them off at soil level, usually the best method when thinning root crops. A thorough watering beforehand reduces the risk of injuring the roots of the remaining seedlings, and a second watering helps to resettle the soil around them afterwards. I try to avoid thinning crops during the middle of the day if temperatures are high, or in windy weather. Start the thinning process as soon as the seedlings are large enough to handle.

Using a seedbed

Some vegetables are best started off in a seedbed, a small patch set aside for raising seedlings that can be transplanted later to their final growing position. This is a useful method for many of the brassicas and other crops that have a long growing period. A seedbed sowing allows you to use the garden space allocated to them to produce other, faster-maturing crops in the meantime. If you are using a seedbed, create it in an open position, working the soil to a fine tilth, and make sure you keep it well watered and weeded so that the developing plants do not suffer any checks in growth. Just before transplanting, water the area well so that plenty of soil clings to each rootball and the roots suffer as little disturbance or damage as possible.

Sowing Seed Inside

Sowing inside in pots, trays, or cells, helps to get crops off to an early start. It is useful when the weather is poor or simply unpredictable, and it is essential for half-hardy vegetables, such as tomatoes, that need a long growing season.

INDOOR SOWING can be used for a variety of crops. I sowed early brassicas in cells (*above picture*) since my heavy soil was far too wet and cold for them to be sown direct into the ground. For half-hardy crops, such as tomatoes, peppers, aubergines, and melons, which need time for the fruits to ripen, raising plants inside is the only reliable method. It is useful, too, for beans and courgettes, which can then be planted out as soon as frosts are over. Warmth is easily applied to aid germination, and seedlings won't be ravaged by slugs and snails.

Preparing compost & sowing

Depending on what you are growing, you can use a selection of different-sized trays, small pots, or cells. If you are sowing seeds that require heat, such as tomatoes, peppers, and aubergines, a heated propagator is a must – there is a huge assortment to choose from (including unheated types as well). I use a multipurpose compost, but special seed composts are also available, if you prefer. Sieving it produces the best results but, if time is short, I find you can get away with sieving just the surface layer into the tray or pot. I like to work with dry or only slightly dampened compost and then, once the seeds have been sown, allow the compost to soak up all the moisture it needs from the bottom.

Gently firm the compost in the tray or pot, but take care not to compact it. The seed packet will make clear the depth to which the seed should be sown, the temperature needed, and any other requirements, and it really does pay to heed this

SOWING IN TRAYS

1 *Space seed that is large enough to handle* (here, tomato) *at regular intervals on lightly firmed compost.*

2 *Using a pointed dibber or pencil, push each seed just below the surface, and cover with compost.*

3 *If mixing varieties within a tray, label each as soon as you have sown the row to avoid later confusion.*

4 *Stand the tray in a container of clean water until the compost has soaked up sufficient moisture.*

advice carefully. Sow as sparsely as possible to make thinning less of a chore, and to produce healthy, sturdy seedlings. Sown too densely, they become weak and straggly, and often make poor plants.

I always use mains water for seeds and seedlings. Water from a butt is extremely useful in the garden, but with delicate seedlings, you run the risk of introducing damping-off disease. Avoid using really cold water, which may give seedlings a nasty shock.

Put the pots or trays in a propagator and stand it in a greenhouse or on a windowsill that receives plenty of natural light. The propagator may be heated or unheated, according to the seeds' needs. As soon as the seedlings emerge they will need more natural light and should be moved out. If you have a greenhouse or cold frame, this is often the best place for them, but check the plants' temperature requirements first. Try to acclimatize the seedlings gradually. If there is space, I like to leave them in the unheated propagator for a day before taking them out. I use a combination of sunny windowsills and cold frames to grow on the seedlings. On a sill, you will doubtless be fighting a battle against them becoming etiolated (pale and drawn). Choosing the sunniest sill possible, or standing trays or pots on aluminium foil, with a backdrop of foil, will help.

The advantages of cells

Sowing in cell units allows seedlings to form particularly good root systems that won't be damaged during pricking out. It is a good idea to sow two or three seeds per cell and thin out all but the most vigorous early on. For calabrese, I used cells in a self-watering propagator – a simple device that produced excellent plants (*right*). A tray of cells stands on wet capillary matting, allowing seedlings to soak up all the moisture they need without the compost becoming saturated. Take care with watering if using an ordinary cell unit – it is easy to let the cells on the edge get too dry.

From cell to soil

With no competition or risk of damage in pricking out, seedlings in cells produce strong root systems and can be planted straight into the ground after hardening off.

The pricking out stage
Using a dibber, ease out the seedlings (*here, tomatoes*) and lower them carefully into pots of fresh compost. Hold them only by the seed leaves – the first, lowest pair – or you may damage the plant.

Space to grow

As soon as seedlings in trays or pots are large enough to handle, they need pricking out to give them more room to grow. Water well to minimize root damage and prepare pots of fresh compost with ready-dibbed holes. Use a dibber (or pencil) to lift the seedlings and firm the compost around their roots in the new pots. Water the plants in gently. Keep out of full sun for a day or two, then give them as much light as possible while they develop.

Before planting out, thoroughly harden off all young plants. Even those that are completely hardy can suffer a setback if given too sudden a change in environment. A cold frame is extremely useful for getting them acclimatized, but do make sure that temperatures inside never drop too low. During the day, in warm weather, I remove the lids from the cold frame or even take out the plants, but it is essential to put them back in the early evening. When planting out, try to avoid very windy, cold, or hot days as these can all cause stress. The ground should be moist but not wet and, afterwards, water the plants in thoroughly to ensure that the soil is well settled around their roots. As when sowing outside, pegging out a line helps to produce a satisfyingly straight row.

NATURAL CROP PROTECTION

Protecting your crops pays dividends, no matter what size your garden. Fleece, cloches, cold frames, or a greenhouse all help to extend the growing season, allowing you to bring plants to maturity earlier and keep them cropping for longer.

THERE ARE MANY WAYS of protecting crops. At the very start of the season, you can encourage an early harvest by using cloches, polythene sheets, bell jars (*above*), or fleece to warm the soil before you sow. By the time outside temperatures start to rise, your plants will already be well established. At the end of the year, winter salad crops benefit from protection, too. It extends their season, helps to minimize the battering effect of heavy rain or hail, and produces more tender leaves. As long as they receive sufficient light and water, some crops, such as carrots, can be kept covered right through until harvest time, with the added benefit of keeping potential pests at bay.

Following tradition
Glass lantern lights look stylish and, because they are easy to ventilate, create good growing conditions.

Temporary cover

Usually the least expensive way of protecting crops is to use temporary structures. These have the advantage that they are easy to move from area to area and also take up little storage space. I'm a great fan of bell jars and lantern lights because they look attractive as well as being extremely effective. If possible, use those that allow you to change the amount of ventilation according to the weather and the plants' needs. If the air beneath is allowed to get too warm or muggy, plants soon suffer, diseases and pests build up and plants may even die.

Glass, polythene, and double-skinned polycarbonate sheeting are commonly used in cloches of all kinds (and in cold frames) and should all allow adequate light through to the plants. I prefer glass, but it is the easiest to break and can be heavy to move. The range of cloche styles is huge. Most are fairly simple to assemble, but a few test both ingenuity and temper. If you have the opportunity, check before you buy.

PIPPA'S ORGANIC TIPS

■ Fleece and cloches will protect crops against pests such as carrot fly and slugs. Make sure plants under plastic or glass are kept well watered.

■ Recycle household waste The bottom half of a clear plastic drinks bottle up-ended over a seedling – for instance, a courgette – makes an inexpensive mini-cloche. Old newspapers make good cover for newly emerged crops, such as potatoes, when frost is forecast.

◁ **Into the tunnel**
Warmth and protection from wind in early spring will help these young lettuce plants to grow stronger and faster. This concertina-style polytunnel folds flat for easy storage.

△ **Covering of fleece**
Fleece creates a snug environment for strawberry plants, while still letting through light and water. It can be left in place until the fruits form and need to ripen.

Fleece and perforated plastic films should provide a couple of degrees of frost protection when spread over young crops. Although they won't improve the look of the garden, they do have the advantage of being inexpensive and totally portable as well as allowing good air circulation. Sheets of newspaper, even old net curtains, also work well but, like fleece and sheeting, they need to be well anchored so that they cannot blow away. Secure them with some bricks or stones, or dig the edges into the soil.

Cold frames & greenhouses

A cold frame is really useful, allowing you to raise seedlings in a protected environment, harden off young plants before planting out, and even grow some crops, such as lettuce, inside for their whole season. However, the relatively low height will restrict what you can grow. If you have sufficient space (and funds), a greenhouse will do all that and much more, especially if you can heat it in some way. You can choose from a huge array of shapes and sizes, from a miniature lean-to to something resembling one of the gigantic structures at London's Kew Gardens. Prices vary enormously and, to a large extent, you get what you pay for in terms of size and quality. I would advise buying the largest greenhouse, or cold frame, you can afford. It is astonishing how quickly you will fill every inch of space.

It is important that a greenhouse has adequate vents in the roof and sides, as without them plants soon overheat in summer, and poor ventilation also encourages pests and diseases. Watch for this in the cheaper models, as it can be appallingly poor. Check, too, that the structure itself is sufficiently sturdy to withstand winter winds, as you need something that will last as long as possible and not collapse in a mangled heap after a single season.

Remember, too, that whatever kind of protection you give, you must ensure that bees have easy access to plants, at least during the warmest part of the day. Pollinating insects must be able to reach the flowers of crops such as tomatoes, peppers, melons, and aubergines if they are to fertilize them.

First potatoes (*overleaf*) A covering of clear polythene, until the earthing-up stage, helps to produce an extra-early crop of tubers.

GOOD CULTIVATION

Keeping your kitchen garden well maintained will ensure that you get the best from your plot. Clearing weeds before they set seed saves work in future years, and making sure that plants receive sufficient water helps to achieve the maximum crop.

THE AMOUNT OF WATER that fruit and vegetables require varies from crop to crop and season to season, and also depends on a plant's stage of development. But suffice to say, during summer everything is likely to be growing fast and in need of a regular supply. While dealing with weeds, you can keep a look-out for pests and diseases (*see pp.32–35*) and crops that are nearly ready to pick. Protect ripening fruit from birds, and keep strawberries free of mud splashes, which may encourage mould, by tucking straw under the plants (*above picture*).

Fruitful mulch
Mulch around plants such as strawberries with well-rotted manure or other organic matter. Conserving moisture will result in good crops, since the fruits need water if they are to swell properly.

Adequate moisture

Do all you can to conserve water, even in summers when there are no restrictions in force. Installing a water butt, or preferably more than one, allows you to use as much rain or recycled water as possible. With a water diverter fitted to the downpipe from the bathroom, you should have a plentiful supply, even during spells of dry weather.

Any bulky organic matter incorporated into the soil will help to retain moisture, but also consider mulching – it works just as well in a vegetable plot as it does in a flower bed. I mulched my fruit trees, strawberries, and raspberries with well-rotted manure as soon as I planted them, then renewed it as necessary. Remember that to be effective a mulch needs to be at least 5–7.5cm (2–3in) deep and applied to moist soil. Planting in a slight depression, or carefully making one around the bases of trees or bushes, will also help to conserve water and channel it towards the plants' roots – particularly useful if your garden is on a slope, with a quick run-off. If you scoop away soil after planting, take care not to damage or expose underlying roots.

Except in times of real crisis, you should try to water in the early evening or, failing that, very early morning. This will dramatically reduce the water lost by evaporation from the soil surface. If you water towards the end of the day, plants will have plenty of time to drink it up before temperatures rise again.

In small areas, a watering can may well be adequate and this certainly ensures the least wastage. You can apply the water only where it is needed, directly at the base of the plant where it will soak straight down to the roots. In a large garden like mine, however, it would probably mean installing floodlights so that I could water well into the middle of the night. Here, a hosepipe is the best solution. Sprinklers are terribly wasteful, watering the areas between plants as thoroughly as the plants themselves. (It is estimated that a sprinkler uses as much water in one hour as a family of four uses in a whole day.) Sprinklers may also cause capping of the soil surface, encouraging run-off and further waste.

If you use a hose, apply the water gently, using a "rose" fitting, and make sure that you direct the water towards the bases of the plants that need it, rather than showering the whole bed. If the soil has become very dry, I like first to water all the areas that need it with a gentle sprinkling, then water the whole area again immediately afterwards, but this time more thoroughly. The first watering dampens the surface and allows better penetration on the second, more extensive application.

Check the weeds

If you do not keep a look out for weeds (*see p.17*) and remove them at regular intervals, they too will use up a lot water, to the detriment of your crops. Weeds will also compete, often very successsfully, for nutrients and may harbour pests and diseases. Once the crops are in the ground, hoe off weeds, or carefully fork or pull them out by hand. In hot, dry weather they will soon die if left on the surface, but leave them there only if they are still young and show no signs of setting seed.

On a recently cleared piece of ground like mine, a few perennial weeds are bound to shoot up, some of them, such as docks, potentially quite large. Ideally, these should be removed, roots included, but, if they are growing close to your crops and the

Remove the competition
Try to remove weeds while they are as small as possible to avoid disturbing the roots of neighbouring vegetables, and before the weeds have a chance to self-sow another generation.

weather is very dry, you can simply cut off their foliage as soon as it appears. This way you avoid disturbing crop roots and yet temporarily halt the competition. Once the vegetables have been harvested, dig out the weed, roots and all. Mulches, usually applied largely to conserve water, should also have a weed-suppressing effect, another good reason for laying them as soon as possible.

Need to feed?

Even if you keep the plot free of weeds and have prepared the soil well before planting and sowing, you may need to apply fertilizer at some stage while the crops are growing. There are several organic fertilizers available, but remember that the most important thing is to improve the soil's structure and fertility before you sow or plant, using well-rotted manure or garden compost. Without this, most fertilizers will be of limited benefit because soil won't be able to hold on to them for long. Pelleted poultry manure is readily available and easy to apply but make sure it is from an organic source. Comfrey is extremely effective (*see p.19*). Magnesium deficiency, indicated by yellowing or other discolouration between leaf veins, starting on the lower or older leaves, can be counteracted by using Epsom salts.

PIPPA'S ORGANIC TIPS

■ An organic mulch will help to conserve moisture, gradually improve soil structure as worms take it down into the soil, and, depending what material you use, may add nutrients. It needs to be at least 5–7.5cm (2–3in) deep and applied to moist soil.

■ Water at the base of plants. I try to lift large, closely packed leaves, like those of a courgette, to avoid getting the foliage, flowers, or developing fruits wet, since this can encourage some types of disease.

■ If fertilizers are to give maximum benefit, the soil itself must be improved first with manure or garden compost.

BASIC PRUNING

There is nothing difficult about growing fruit trees but,

if you want them to produce good crops of evenly ripened

fruit, some pruning will be needed. This will also help to keep

the trees relatively free of pests and diseases.

AN OLD GNARLED tree that has been left to its own devices certainly looks lovely, and will continue to bear fruit, but it is unlikely to crop as well as one that has been pruned regularly. Apples and pears seem to benefit from pruning more than plums and cherries, and on these it is best kept to a minimum to reduce the risk of introducing silver leaf disease.

The reason why

Pruning encourages a tree to grow in the shape you require. This is obviously important for cordons, fans, and espaliers, but even if, like me, you are growing the majority as bushes, some pruning is still needed. Removing excessive growth helps to keep the tree open in the centre, reducing the risk of disease while also ensuring that it makes an attractive shape and

Pruning out old wood
Encourage mature trees to make more productive growth by cutting out old wood that has ceased to crop well. Prune back to a strong new shoot.

Cut to a bud
In routine pruning, make each cut close to a healthy, outward-facing bud, angling it so that rain will not accumulate and possibly encourage disease.

allows fruit to ripen. Diseases, such as canker (*see p.79*), should always be removed as part of the pruning routine because, if left, they are likely to spread and cause further damage. Similarly, any damaged or crossing branches should be pruned out. Put diseased wood straight in the bin or burn it as some of the canker diseases are particularly resilient.

Although the ultimate size of a tree is largely determined by its rootstock, pruning can help you to keep a potentially large tree within reasonable bounds, or at least at a height that allows you to pick the fruit.

How & when

To keep the shape of a tree's crown well balanced you will always need to prune vigorous shoots quite lightly and weak ones much harder. This may appear perverse, but hard pruning results in more vigorous growth with relatively few fruit buds. These will all then be sufficiently well-fuelled to produce good-sized fruits. A lightly pruned shoot will make only a small amount of new growth.

With apples and pears, most pruning is carried out during the winter, while for plums, cherries, and other stone fruits, any pruning needs to be done in summer, to avoid the potentially fatal silver leaf disease (*see p.81*). Pruning cuts should always be kept as small as possible so that potential disease entry points are kept to a minimum. Always use a really sharp pair of secateurs (or a small saw for larger scale pruning) as blunt blades make poor cuts, often damaging the remaining wood in the process. If larger branches need to be removed on an established tree, prune back to the branch collar (the slight swelling where one branch meets another or the trunk). This minimizes the risk of die-back.

Most commonly grown apples are described as spur-bearers (*see below*). A few varieties, however, produce their fruit on the shoot tips and are known as tip-bearers (for example, 'Kerry Pippin'). Check the catalogue or plant label when you buy. More common are partial tip-bearers, which include

'Discovery' and 'Bramley's Seedling'. Pruning an established tip-bearer consists largely of taking out old wood that has already fruited to encourage new shoots to form, and tip-pruning branch leaders to stop them breaking under the apples' weight and to make them form fruit-bearing shoots. Prune partial tip-bearers rather like a spur-bearer, cutting back strong laterals, more than 20–25cm (8–10in) long, to five or six buds. Leave shorter laterals unpruned.

PRUNING AN APPLE BUSH

Pruning on planting

An apple bush is one of the easiest, most useful tree forms to grow and is just as suitable for pears and plums. Bushes have a short trunk (about 60–75cm (24–30in) tall, from which the branches radiate. The aim is to create an open crown. On planting, prune the leader to just above the topmost of 3–4 strong laterals, and shorten the laterals by two-thirds of their length. (Training may have already been started on some trees you buy, and the leader removed.)

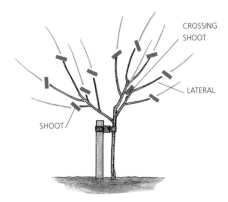

Year 2, winter

Select the laterals you want to become the main branches, to create a good open shape, and shorten them by half. Prune other shoots to 4–5 buds, and take out crossing or badly placed shoots.

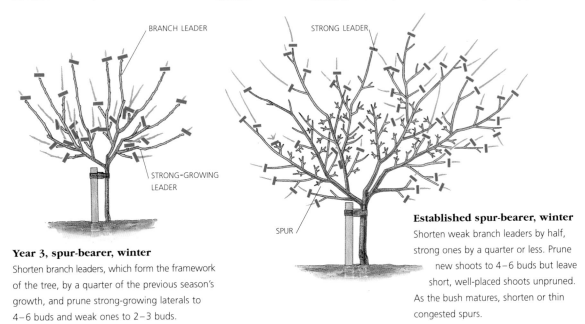

Year 3, spur-bearer, winter

Shorten branch leaders, which form the framework of the tree, by a quarter of the previous season's growth, and prune strong-growing laterals to 4–6 buds and weak ones to 2–3 buds.

Established spur-bearer, winter

Shorten weak branch leaders by half, strong ones by a quarter or less. Prune new shoots to 4–6 buds but leave short, well-placed shoots unpruned. As the bush matures, shorten or thin congested spurs.

PEST & DISEASE PREVENTION

However carefully you look after your plants, you are bound to have a few problems, mainly in the form of pests or diseases. It is important to check for these on a regular basis, so that they can be dealt with quickly and the damage minimized.

ALTHOUGH PESTS AND DISEASES are never going to be welcome guests in your garden, it is important to keep things in perspective. Any creature that you find creeping or crawling over crops is not necessarily an enemy, indeed it could be an ally, a potential predator or parasite of pests. Be aware of the most common problems likely to affect vegetables and fruit (*see overleaf*) and you may be able to avoid them altogether by taking preventative action.

The common-sense approach

Whether you use chemicals or are gardening organically, the same principles apply: make regular patrols and think before you act. Sometimes pests may indeed be causing damage, but that damage may not be significant and certainly not sufficient to merit taking control measures. Being on the alert to

Deter cabbage root fly
To prevent this fly from laying its eggs, buy or make discs or squares, 10cm (4in) wide, from card or carpet underlay. Fit them around the bases of brassica seedlings immediately after planting out.

potential problems means that you can pick off pests or infected leaves and also remove any debris which could harbour pests or diseases.

It is a simple but fairly reliable rule that insects that move speedily are generally harmless to plants (they move fast because they need to be able to catch their food), and those which move slowly are more likely to be plant, or perhaps debris, eaters. If unsure, wait before you take any action. Make sure that any creature you find close to the damage is actually responsible for it. Earwigs and woodlice, for instance, are often wrongly blamed for attacking tree fruits. In reality, they are usually hiding away in already damaged fruit, and you may, instead, have a wasp problem. If so, you may decide to make a trap (*above picture*) by half-filling a jar with beer. Cover with paper and pierce a hole in the top.

Many organic gardeners are happy to use sprays based on derris and soap-based insecticides, and certain fungicides based on copper or sulphur, but it is worth remembering that these are not always specific in their action. A soap-based insecticide may kill not only the pests but also beneficial or harmless creatures. Wherever possible, I avoid using products such as these and try to do all I can to prevent problems, or at least keep damage to a minimum.

You can often choose vegetable varieties that are resistant to specific pests or diseases, or at least are able to tolerate the damage they cause. The range varies from year to year so look through several seed catalogues to see just what is available. Some pests are more troublesome at certain times of the season, and you may be able to reduce or eliminate damage

Keep out the birds

A low netting tunnel is more effective at protecting a row of newly sown peas from birds than humming or buzzing tapes, which, like scarecrows, soon lose their effectiveness.

simply by sowing or planting earlier, or by choosing a variety that flowers or fruits at a time when there are fewer pests about. In my newly cultivated soil, I knew wireworms were likely to be a problem but, by concentrating on early potatoes, I managed to limit damage, and also gave the slugs less chance to feast.

If pests are known to detect host plants by smell, it helps to grow strongly aromatic plants close by. I grew carrots and onions close to each other to deter both carrot fly and onion fly. Some gardeners swear by the benefits of growing French marigolds near plants susceptible to whitefly.

Barriers & traps

Some pests fly, walk, or crawl in and attack the plants themselves; others lay eggs that then hatch out to produce young that cause the damage. Put a barrier in the way and they have to go elsewhere. The specific requirements vary from pest to pest (*see overleaf*), but horticultural fleece is extremely useful

against a wide range. I use it to deter aphids and caterpillars, to name but a few. With calabrese it brings the bonus of keeping cabbage root fly at bay. When laying fleece, make sure it is well anchored, so that pests cannot enter via the base. Brassica collars can be fitted to plants susceptible to cabbage root fly (*see facing page*). For low-flying carrot fly, a fine mesh, clear polythene, or fleece "fence" around the crop should keep the carrots damage-free.

For my plot, rabbit-netting was essential (*see p.14*) but you could also fit rabbit guards around young trees or bushes, or make small chicken-wire fences around individual beds. Birds can be a menace, too (*see overleaf*). Keep them off seed with a net tunnel, or twiggy sticks and zigzagged thread (*see p.21*).

Some pests are fairly easy to trap: saucers of beer attract slugs (or milk works just as well, especially if you add a sprinkling of grain or porridge oats). You can also repel slugs with a spray containing extract of yucca, or adhesive copper strips. These can be laid on the soil, but work best around a container.

Encourage predators

Protect natural predators such as ladybirds and their larvae (*below*), hoverflies, lacewings (*bottom*), and carabid and devils' coach horse beetles, and tempt them into your garden. Open-centred flowers such as phacelia and the poached egg plant  (*Limnanthes douglasii*) look pretty and will attract hoverflies. You can buy or make shelters where lacewings can safely overwinter, and never be tempted to stamp on fast-scuttling black beetles – they are most likely to be beneficial carabids.

Biological controls are available for some pests (*see p.93*) including *Encarsia formosa* (a parasitic wasp) for glasshouse whitefly, *Aphidius* (a parasitic wasp) and *Aphidoletes* (a predatory midge) for aphids, *Phytoseiulus persimilis* (a predatory mite) for red spider mite, and nematode controls for vine weevils and slugs. Except for vine weevil and slug controls, these are best introduced into a greenhouse, but all work well and can be used in conjunction with one another to provide totally organic pest control.

COMMON PESTS IN THE KITCHEN GARDEN

Aphids

Greenfly and blackfly may cause distortion and discolouration, and possibly spread virus infections as they feed. Use a strong jet of water to clear infestations; encourage natural predators (*see previous page*); raise plants under fleece; consider biological controls in a greenhouse, or a soap-based insecticide for outdoor plants.

Birds

May eat buds on fruit trees and peck fruits, uproot onion sets, eat seeds, and shred foliage. Plant fruit in a cage or net individual plants (*see p.15*); put up a scarecrow, buzzing or humming tapes, or a net tunnel (*see previous page*); use twiggy sticks and taut thread (*see p.21*).

Cabbage root fly

Can damage all brassicas including calabrese, broccoli, turnips, and swedes; seedlings and transplants are particularly vulnerable. Legless maggots eat or bore into the roots. Fit collars (*see previous page*) when planting seedlings, or cover crops with fleece.

Carrot fly

Carrots, parsnips, and celery may be attacked as the maggots tunnel into roots. Delay sowing carrots until early summer to reduce the problem; carrots harvested before late summer will also show less damage. Rotate crops; raise under fleece; sow sparsely; choose less susceptible varieties.

Caterpillars

There are many different types, often allied to specific plants. They eat mainly foliage but some tunnel into fruits. Hand-picking works well but needs repeating frequently; the bacterial insecticide containing *Bacillus thuringiensis* can be used, or cover crops with fleece or fine netting to prevent adults from laying eggs.

Flea beetles

Tiny beetles leave numerous grazed areas or holes in foliage. Leaves turn brown in extreme cases and seedlings may be killed. Sow when weather and soil conditions ensure rapid growth so that seedlings are better able to tolerate an attack; raise plants under fleece. Brassicas and rocket are susceptible.

Mice

Will steal seeds and nibble young shoots, corn cobs, and fruits and seeds in store. Keep seeds in mouse-proof containers; set traps; protect newly sown seed with bell cloches or upturned sections of plastic bottles.

Onion fly

Leeks and shallots may be attacked, but onions are most susceptible. Maggots eat roots and may tunnel into onion bulbs; plants may die. Grow onions from sets, which are less prone to attack; destroy infested plants promptly before the maggots move into the soil to pupate; rotate crops.

Red spider mite

Minute yellow or white flecks develop on leaves, you may see very fine webbing, and severely damaged leaves turn brown and dry. Infestations are encouraged by hot, dry air so try to increase moisture levels in a greenhouse and mist foliage with water; use biological control (*see previous page*).

Slugs and snails

Hunt and dispose of these when soil or plants are wet or at night-time. Create pine-needle or cocoa-shell barriers; set traps or use repellents (*see previous page*); use biological control (slugs only).

Whitefly

Numerous tiny white flies take wing as you approach affected plants. With glasshouse whitefly, plants may become sticky due to the insects' sugary excreta (honeydew). Use biological control such as *Encarsia formosa* or the predatory beetle *Delphastus* if the infestation is severe. Unfortunately, biological control is not suitable for brassica whitefly. Use a soap-based insecticide or learn to live with the problem.

Wireworm

Orange-brown larvae of the click beetle tunnel into vegetables such as carrots and potatoes and attack seedling bases. They are especially troublesome in land recently cultivated from grassland, but should disappear after three or four years. Lift crops as early as possible.

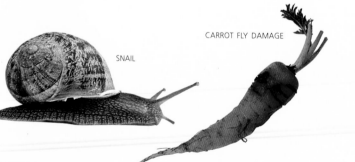

SNAIL

CARROT FLY DAMAGE

CATERPILLARS
AND THE DAMAGE
THEY CAUSE

POSSIBLE DISEASES & DISORDERS

Apple and pear canker
Can sometimes affect fruit trees (*see p.79*) but it is possible to prune it out.

Blossom end rot
Black, leathery, sunken patches develop at the blossom end of tomatoes or peppers, although the rest of the plant (and often the remainder of the fruit) appears perfectly normal. The disorder is caused by a shortage of calcium in the fruits, encouraged by inadequate or erratic watering. Keep plants, especially those in containers, well watered so that the compost always stays just moist.

Clubroot
Affects brassicas, whose roots become swollen and distorted so that plants fail to thrive. Lime the soil (*see p.19*) and improve drainage; choose resistant varieties; raise plants in individual pots for planting out since sturdy seedlings with good root systems are better able to cope with the disease; destroy infected or suspect plants, never compost them.

Damping off; foot and root rots
The stem base darkens and withers and seedlings or plants die off; fungal growth is sometimes apparent. The problem is encouraged by poor hygiene, use of non-mains water, and re-using contaminated potting compost. Use only mains water on seedlings; rotate crops; use fresh compost; consider watering seedlings with a copper-based fungicide.

Downy mildew
Slightly fluffy, off-white fungal growth appears usually on lower leaf surfaces. Brassicas, lettuce, and onions are prone to attack. Pick off affected areas; improve air circulation by making sure that plants are not overcrowded and by removing debris and weeds.

Grey mould
Fuzzy grey fungal patches appear on any part of a plant above ground. The fungus (*Botrytis*) is encouraged by poor hygiene and cool, damp conditions. Remove debris and damaged parts regularly; avoid wetting foliage unnecessarily when watering.

Potato common scab
Scabby patches develop on the skin but the rest of the tuber is unaffected and is still edible. Incorporate plenty of organic matter prior to planting and do not lime soil; water regularly; choose resistant varieties.

Potato and tomato blight
Potatoes and outdoor tomatoes are prone in damp, muggy weather. Foliage browns and dies, potato haulms (stems) may be killed, and fruits or tubers develop brown discolouration, usually followed by rotting. Avoid susceptible varieties; try to improve air circulation by spacing plants well and giving them an open position. Remove affected parts promptly and bin or burn them; rotate crops; consider using a copper fungicide.

Powdery mildew
Attacks a wide range of plants, including brassicas and courgettes, and is worst in dry weather. Powdery white fungal growth appears mainly on upper leaf surfaces. Keep plants well watered as dry soil encourages the infection; improve air circulation by spacing plants well, keeping them weed-free, and removing debris.

Rusts
Bright orange or dark brown spores appear usually on the undersides of leaves and often cause yellowing. It is especially common on leeks and plums. Pick off affected areas; improve air circulation (*as above*); avoid wetting foliage; avoid excessive use of high-nitrogen fertilizers, such as poultry manure; dress the soil with rock potash before planting out or sowing.

Silver leaf
A serious disease that affects stone fruit, such as plums and cherries (*see p.81*).

Viruses
Foliage becomes flecked, ringed, or streaked with yellow, and plants are often distorted and stunted; they may even die. There is no cure, so bin or burn plants promptly. Choose resistant varieties where available (for instance, for cucumbers, courgettes, and marrows). Try to control aphids and other sap-feeding pests since these may be responsible for spreading viruses.

POTATO COMMON SCAB

BLOSSOM END ROT

EFFECTS OF CLUBROOT

TOMATO BLIGHT

VEGETABLES

& HERBS

I firmly believe that you should grow the foods that you really enjoy eating. The vegetables and herbs that follow are my personal selection. They have been grouped according to the part of the plant that is eaten – lettuce with the leaf vegetables, for instance, carrots and leeks with the root and stem crops, and so forth.

LEAF & SALAD VEGETABLES

Spinach & chard

These leafy vegetables not only taste good, but some could be grown for their looks alone. Ruby chard, for instance, with its deep green and bright red colour, is a star of the ornamental kitchen garden, or even the flower bed. Some of the names can be confusing. True spinach is not related to chard; however, the crop variously known as spinach beet, perpetual spinach, or leaf beet is. Spinach beet has finer midribs than chard, but a coarser taste than true spinach. I use both spinach and chard raw in salads, or cook them in stir-fries and Italian dishes.

SITE AND SOIL Sun or partial shade and fertile, moisture-retentive soil.
SOWING OUTDOORS Mid-spring to early summer for chards and summer spinach, and late summer to early autumn for winter spinach. A mid- to late-summer sowing of spinach beet yields a winter crop. Sow chard and spinach beet 2.5cm (1in) deep and 10cm (4in) apart in rows 30cm (12in) apart; sow spinach in 2.5cm (1in) deep drills that are spaced 30cm (12in) apart.
FINAL PLANTING DISTANCE Thin chard and spinach beet to about 30cm (12in) apart. Thin spinach seedlings to about 7.5cm (3in) apart, then again a few weeks later to about 15cm (6in) apart.
HARVESTING Midsummer to late autumn for chards. With a careful choice of varieties, spinach can be picked for most of the year.
APPROXIMATE YIELD About 3kg (7lb) per 3m (10ft) row.

Keys to success

■ Manure the ground well because, if spinach does not have plenty to feed on, crops tend to be poor with an unpleasant, bitter taste.
■ If you find spinach difficult to grow because your garden is too dry or too warm, try white-stemmed Swiss chard or spinach beet, since these are far less likely to bolt (run to seed) and often succeed where spinach will not.
■ Spinach and chard benefit from regular weeding and watering, plus the use of a mulch to help keep the soil moist and the leaves tender.

"Sow summer spinach between your sweet corn plants. The partial shade cast by the taller crop suits it well."

■ A mid- to late-summer sowing of spinach beet should allow you to harvest small amounts of young leaves throughout the winter and spring, especially if you give plants protection from mid-autumn onwards.
■ Harvest either vegetable by carefully cutting off the outer leaves, or by slicing off the entire head about 2.5cm (1in) above ground level and leaving the stump in the soil to resprout for use as a cut-and-come-again crop.

Scarlet splash The red stems of ruby chard make it the most eye-catching of vegetables. ▷

Traditional lettuce

Although my kitchen garden may seem huge, especially when viewed through the distorting eye of the TV camera, I soon found I was short of space. Rather than setting aside special areas, I decided to grow lettuce in any spare patches and intersow the seed with slow-growing crops such as parsnips. The choice of lettuce varieties is enormous, ranging from large, crisp, iceberg types to soft, sweet butterheads and slender, long-leaved cos. Grow a selection, including some green- and red-leaved loose-leaf lettuce (*see overleaf*), so that your salads combine colour, flavour, and texture.

> " Lettuce will appreciate a place in one of the moister, cooler parts of the garden, and can even tolerate a little shade. "

Thin out seedlings
To avoid disturbing the remaining seedlings when thinning out rows, water the soil really well beforehand, and again when you have finished.

SITE AND SOIL Moisture-retentive soil with plenty of organic matter dug in, in a sunny or partially shaded site.

SOWING OUTDOORS For summer crops, make successional sowings from early spring to midsummer. Sow seed about 1cm (½in) deep, in rows 30cm (12in) apart. Thin out as soon as the first true leaves appear, and then at intervals to reach the spacing given below.

SOWING INDOORS For a winter crop in a cold frame or greenhouse, sow under glass from autumn to midwinter, depending on variety.

FINAL PLANTING DISTANCE 15–30cm (6–12in), depending on variety.

HARVESTING Throughout summer; also during winter for suitable varieties grown with protection.

APPROXIMATE YIELD 10–20 heads per 3m (10ft) row.

Keys to success

■ Lettuce seed dislikes very high temperatures. Above 21°C (70°F), the rate of germination will be greatly reduced, so it is best to avoid sowing during the warmest times of the year.

■ To get a lot of lettuce fairly quickly and in a small space, choose a cos variety (such as 'Kendo' or 'Little Gem') and sow the seed about 2.5cm (1in) apart, in rows about 10cm (4in) apart. Don't thin the seedlings, but when the closely packed rows of lettuces are about five weeks old, cut each plant back to leave a stump 2–2.5cm (¾–1in) high. In about six weeks, the cut stumps should have resprouted to give a reasonable second crop.

■ Slugs can be a nightmare. I suggest using biological controls, or you can try using barriers or traps (*see pp.33–34*).

"For a continuous supply, make successional sowings every two weeks, as soon as the seedlings from the previous sowing emerge."

■ Raising seedlings in cells or modules helps to avoid slug damage in the early stages. This works well in spring and early summer, but transplanting them successfully once the weather turns warm can be difficult.

■ Aphids can be a problem. Covering the seedlings as soon as they emerge with horticultural fleece will prevent aphids from landing on the crop, but unfortunately it may also increase the risk of grey mould disease.

Moisture lovers

Lettuce need a regular supply of water to prevent the leaves from becoming tough and the plants from bolting (running to seed).

Loose-leaf lettuce

For fashionably colourful salads, with interesting textures, you need to grow a selection of loose-leaf lettuces. The range of available varieties grows every year, but already includes lettuces in just about every shade of purple and green, with a huge variation in the degree of crimping or curling.

SITE AND SOIL Moisture-retentive soil in sun or partial shade. Purple varieties colour best in sun.
SOWING OUTDOORS Sow in succession from early spring to midsummer, 1cm (½in) deep, in rows about 30cm (12in) apart. Thin to give the spacing below.
SOWING INDOORS Sow in autumn for a winter crop grown under glass.
FINAL PLANTING DISTANCE 25–30cm (10–12in), depending on variety.
HARVESTING With protection, through most of the year.
APPROXIMATE YIELD 10–20 heads per 3m (10ft) row.

Keys to success

■ Growing methods are the same as for ordinary lettuces (*see previous page*), but because loose-leaf lettuces don't form a heart, they are often easier than traditional butterhead, cos, or iceberg types and generally are not so quick to bolt (run to seed).

■ Some seed companies offer salad-leaf mixtures, sometimes containing a range of lettuces only, and sometimes including other leaves such as rocket. With these mixtures, you can scatter the seed over a patch, rather than sow it in straight drills, and harvest as a cut-and-come-again crop (*see below*). If you prefer, try making a seed mixture of your own favourites.

■ In cool conditions, it is possible to transplant seedlings that have been thinned out, if you want a frilly lettuce or two among your flowers.

■ There are two ways of harvesting. Pick leaves as you need them to obtain a good mix of textures and colours. You will, however, need to keep picking regularly. Alternatively, use as a cut-and-come-again crop, cutting the entire head, while the plants are no more than 10–15cm (4–6in) high, just above the top of the stem and leaving the stump to reshoot.

■ If you gently plunge leaves in cold water immediately after picking and shake off all excess moisture, they will keep reasonably well, in a plastic bag in the salad box of a refrigerator, for a day or two at least.

Prolonged harvest
Loose-leaf lettuces are more successful than other types in less-than-perfect conditions and just a few plants will provide leaves over a long period.

Radicchio

People who claim to dislike the taste of chicory, have, I greatly suspect, unknowingly enjoyed the red-leaved form of chicory known as radicchio. It has become a popular ingredient of many a trendy salad. The leaves have a slightly tough texture and a decidedly bitter flavour, which you either love or hate. It is one of the vegetables that I enjoy, but not in enomous quantities. However, its leaves are so useful for bringing fantastic colour to winter salads that I feel compelled to grow just a few plants in my garden.

SITE AND SOIL Grows well in all but a very heavy and wet soil.
SOWING OUTDOORS Sow direct in drills, 1cm (½in) deep, from mid-spring until late summer. Thin to give spacing below.
SOWING INDOORS In trays or cells from mid-spring until late summer, depending on variety. Plant out from late spring.
FINAL PLANTING DISTANCE 20–30cm (8–12in) apart, depending on variety.
HARVESTING During summer, autumn, and winter, with a range of varieties.

Keys to success

■ Always thoroughly harden off radicchio that has been raised indoors before planting it outside.
■ Radicchio can be used as a cut-and-come-again crop – cut it down to about 2.5cm (1in) above soil level and leave the stump to resprout. Alternatively, pick individual leaves as and when they are needed.
■ For the earliest direct-sown crops, and to prolong the potential harvesting period, cover the crop with fleece, a mini-polytunnel or cloches.

Winter tints
Leaves often don't take on their most eye-catching hues until the weather starts to turn cold.

"Choose late-maturing varieties of radicchio for leaves that can be picked outdoors throughout winter. "

ROCKET

■ The spicy leaves of rocket (also known as roquette and rucola) have become more and more popular in the last few years.
It is is not difficult to grow, requiring a well-fed, moisture-retentive soil in partial shade. If the leaves are to remain tender with a pleasant flavour, regular watering and shade from full sun are essential. Frequent picking also helps, since it encourages plants to produce plenty of succulent new leaves.

■ Make successional sowings from mid-spring to midsummer in drills about 1cm (½in) deep and 30cm (12in) apart. As soon as the plants are large enough to handle, thin them to 15cm (6in) apart.

■ Rocket can also be sown under cloches or low polytunnels, or in a cold frame, to provide you with salad leaves in autumn and into winter.

PIPPA'S SELECTION

'Rossa di Treviso'
Has green leaves that, in cool weather, turn red with white veins.

'Palla Rossa Zorzi Precoce'
Leaves turn a particularly deep red in cold weather.

PODDED & SEED VEGETABLES

Peas & mangetout

PIPPA'S SELECTION

'Delikett'
Sweet flavour; can be picked as a mangetout or shelled when mature.

'Douce Provence'
Round-seeded; hardy, dwarf plants.

'Fortune'
Round-seeded; early and very hardy dwarf; good flavour and freezes well.

'Hurst Green Shaft'
Wrinkle-seeded; wilt and downy mildew resistant; sweet and good for freezing.

'Kelvedon Wonder'
Wrinkle-seeded; pea wilt and mildew resistant; good flavour; freezes well.

'Oregon Sugar Pod'
Very sweet mangetout; heavy cropper.

'Senator'
Wrinkle-seeded; very heavy cropping and freezes well.

'Sugar Snap'
Mangetout type; sweet and very flavoursome; great in stir-fries; pods can be eaten whole or shelled, if preferred, when mature.

Until the last few years, I did not like peas particularly, but now I am a real convert, enjoying mangetout as well as traditional shelling peas in all sorts of dishes, both cooked and raw. Peas that you grow yourself really are something special – the fresh, sweet flavour seems to be lost even in the freezing process and, as far as I am concerned, canned peas are fit only for composting. Grow your own and you can eat them at that perfect stage, just before the sugar in them turns to starch.

When to support
You can put in pea sticks before sowing or as the seedlings emerge, but they need to be in place by the time the plants are 5–7.5cm (2–3in) tall.

SITE AND SOIL Preferably a sunny, open site, with neutral to alkaline soil that is moisture-retentive, but not wet. The soil should be well-fed, but without too high a nitrogen content.

SOWING OUTDOORS Round-seeded (*see below*) from midwinter to early spring, wrinkle-seeded and mangetout from early spring to early summer. Sow seed 2.5–5cm (1–2in) deep in a single drill, or sow three rows, 10cm (4in) apart, in a wide drill (*see p.21*).

FINAL PLANTING DISTANCE Depends on variety, but usually 5–7.5cm (2–3in) between seeds, with rows spaced 60–90cm (2–3ft) apart.

HARVESTING Late spring and summer. Shelling peas are ready when the peas nearly touch each other within the pod; mangetout just as the peas start to develop, usually when pods are about 7.5cm (3in) long.

APPROXIMATE YIELD 3.5–4.5kg (8–10lb) per 3m (10ft) row.

Keys to success

■ Pea seeds may be wrinkled or round. For the hardiest shelling peas, or if your soil is poor, choose round-seeded varieties. These can also be sown in late autumn to overwinter and produce a really early crop, although it is a gamble as the failure rate is much higher than if you sow in spring. Don't be put off by the term "wrinkled". The peas are only wrinkled when dried and are perfectly plump when picked and cooked fresh.

■ Birds and mice can be a problem, particularly just after sowing. A netting tunnel (*see p.33*) or temporary cage of chicken wire placed over the area keeps birds away, but if this seems too ugly use twiggy sticks instead.

■ Most peas need support, whether from netting or pea sticks (*see facing page*), since plants that trail on the ground are an open invitation to slugs and snails. If closely spaced, some smaller varieties with a particularly plentiful supply of tendrils, such as 'Markana' and 'Gemini', need little, if any, support. As they grow, they manage to hold one another up.

> " You are wasting your time if you sow peas into cold, wet soil. Delay sowing until conditions improve. "

■ Peas are rather like sweet peas – the more you pick, the more you get. Leave over-mature pods on plants and production will slow up dramatically.

■ Never grow peas on the same spot for more than a year because they are prone to fungal foot- and root-rot diseases. Even if you are not following a strict rotation system, sow them only on soil that has not been used for peas or beans for at least two years.

■ Like other legumes, peas have nitrogen-fixing bacteria in nodules on their roots. These help to improve soil fertility, so once you have finished harvesting, leave the roots in the ground until they die away naturally.

Ripe for shelling
For flavour and succulence, home-grown peas picked and shelled just before they are to be eaten are beyond compare.

Climbing beans

Runner beans look marvellous in the garden, especially if grown up a wigwam of poles, but eating them can sometimes be a disappointment. However, harvest the beans young – no more than 20cm (8in) long and before they begin to resemble warped green cricket bats – and they taste fantastic, with a splendid texture and no fibrous strings. Climbing French beans are grown in the same ways as runners and crop for a longer period than dwarf French beans. I like them because they are less inclined to become stringy. If you want to produce your own haricot beans to dry for winter use, this is the type you should choose, but you need to allow the pods to ripen fully.

SITE AND SOIL Well-prepared fertile soil that is moisture-retentive but not soggy, in sun. Neutral or slightly acid soils tend to produce the best crops.
SOWING OUTDOORS Late spring to early summer, about 5cm (2in) deep. I sow two seeds at the base of each cane of a wigwam and thin out the less vigorous seedling of the two. .
SOWING INDOORS From mid- to late spring in individual pots. Plant out from late spring to early summer, when the last frosts are over.
FINAL PLANTING DISTANCE 23cm (9in) between plants and, if grown in a double row, about 45cm (18in) between rows.
HARVESTING Summer into early autumn. Regular picking is essential to get a long cropping period.
APPROXIMATE YIELD Varies greatly with the amount of soil preparation, watering, and weather, but about 1kg (2lb 4oz) per runner bean plant and 500g (1lb 2oz) for climbing French beans.

Glory of the garden
When first brought to Europe from their native Mexico, runner beans were grown not for food, but for their decorative flowers.

Keys to success

■ Grow beans up supports such as a wigwam of canes or poles (*see facing page*), and they will look good and crop well. Loosely tie the plants on to the supports when you first plant them out, then they will climb on their own.

"For an even prettier effect, combine beans with a few sweet peas and encourage pollinating insects, too."

■ Well-prepared soil is a must. Dig plenty of well-rotted manure, garden compost, or leaf-mould into the soil to help retain moisture. Manure and compost will also help to increase the crop because they provide nutrients. Theory has it that organic matter must

Dwarf French beans

be added the previous year, but I invariably do it just before I sow or plant and it works perfectly well. In my trials on *Gardeners' World*, good soil preparation made a phenomenal difference to the size of yield.

■ Generous, regular watering is the secret of success, especially if combined with thorough soil preparation.

■ Instead of pollinating runner bean flowers in the normal way, some bees may cut into the back of the flower in search of nectar. They get what they want, but the flowers are not pollinated and the result is a disappointing crop. Bees don't seem to do this to climbing French beans, and white-flowered runners (such as 'Mergoles' or 'White Lady') appear less prone to attack.

■ Never grow beans on the same site for two years in succession – they are prone to soil-borne fungal infections which attack the roots and stem bases.

Structural support

Make sure poles are driven firmly into the ground or the weight of mature, bean-laden plants could bring them down on a wet, gusty day.

Even if your gardening is restricted to a patio, it is worth growing some French beans in a large container. They will have that crisp, melt-in-the-mouth quality that somehow seems to have disappeared from shop-bought beans.

SITE AND SOIL Open, sheltered site, with neutral to slightly acid soil.
SOWING OUTDOORS Mid-spring to early summer, 5cm (2in) deep and 15cm (6in) apart. Wait if soil is very wet or cold, or germination will be erratic.
SOWING INDOORS Early to mid-spring in pots. Plant out after frosts.
FINAL PLANTING DISTANCE About 30cm (12in) apart; thin seedlings as necessary.
HARVESTING Summer.
APPROXIMATE YIELD Variable, but about 3kg (7lb) beans per 3m (10ft) row.

Keys to success

■ If you have a greenhouse, you can "force" a crop of pot-grown beans for a delicious, extra-early harvest.

■ In colder areas, or in a very cold or wet year, raise seedlings indoors in individual pots and plant out after the last frosts. Cloches or horticultural fleece will help to warm soil before sowing outside (*see p.24*).

■ Avoid the usual glut by making successional sowings every few weeks until early summer. Towards the end of the season, cover remaining plants with cloches or fleece to make them crop just that bit longer.

■ Water regularly in dry weather. On dry sites, mulch the soil to conserve as much moisture as possible (*see p.28*).

■ Slugs and snails can be a menace. Propping foliage and pods with twiggy sticks clear of the soil often helps.

"Beans will be ready to pick three to four months after sowing."

PIPPA'S SELECTION

'Delinel'
Fine, stringless beans; heavy crops.

'Nassau'
Stringless, flat-podded beans that develop high on the plant, making them less vulnerable to slugs and disease.

'Primel'
Crisp bean with a scrumptious flavour.

'Purple Queen'
Stringless, dark purple beans turn green when cooked.

Sweet corn

All vegetables deteriorate to some extent in the journey from field to greengrocer or supermarket and the supper table, but sweet corn is more vulnerable than most. Freshly picked, instantly cooked corn on the cob is almost unrecognizable compared with its shop-bought counterpart. As soon as the cob is picked from the plant, the sugars start to convert into starches and the kernels become less juicy. Just one word of warning: I once grew a small block of corn and was watching the cobs fatten with eager anticipation. We managed to enjoy a couple, but before the rest were ready, the local badgers popped over for an impromptu feast.

> *"Because sweet corn is wind-pollinated, it crops better if grown in a block."*

SITE AND SOIL Plenty of sun and a rich, fertile soil, preferably slightly acid, in a reasonably sheltered position.
SOWING OUTDOORS From late spring, setting seeds 2.5cm (1in) deep and 38cm (15in) apart to form a block.
SOWING INDOORS Mid-spring, at 15–18°C (59–64°F), in 2.5cm (1in) cells or 5–7.5cm (2–3in) pots. Harden off before planting out in early summer.
FINAL PLANTING DISTANCE 38cm (15in) between plants; 15cm (6in) for mini sweet corn.
HARVESTING From midsummer to mid-autumn, depending on variety and growing conditions.
APPROXIMATE YIELD Seldom more than one or two cobs per plant.

Seeds of success
To obtain a high rate of germination, it is best to sow freshly bought seed.

Keys to success

■ In all but fairly mild areas, it is best to raise sweet corn indoors (*see p.22*) and plant out in early summer, after risk of frost is over. Cover plants for the first few days with fleece, to give them a further chance to acclimatize.

■ If sowing direct into open ground, sow two or three seeds at each position, to allow for failures and for seeds being eaten by mice or birds. Thin out to leave the strongest seedling at each position. Covering seed with cloches improves the success rate.

■ Pollination is much more successful if sweet corn is grown in a grid pattern. Even if you have room for six plants only, grow them in this way.

■ Supersweet varieties really are sweeter and usually more juicy than the standard varieties, but tend to be less robust. To avoid cross-pollination, which would reduce their sweetness, grow them away from standard varieties.

■ To make maximum use of space, try growing dwarf French beans or salad plants in between sweet corn. Although tall, sweet corn casts little shade and fast-maturing crops should do well in the "borrowed" space.

■ Earth-up the bases of the stems if surface roots appear. This also helps to keep plants stable in windy weather.

■ Sweet corn does not need a lot of watering but, for the best yield, try to keep the crop moist at flowering time and when the kernels are swelling.

■ Harvest cobs when the tassels are just turning brown; don't leave it too long or the sugar in the kernels will start to turn into starch. For the best possible flavour, cook immediately – it really does make a difference.

FRUITING & FLOWERING VEGETABLES

Calabrese & broccoli

PIPPA'S SELECTION

'Claret'
Heavy-cropping broccoli with large wine-coloured spears.

'Mercedes'
Calabrese with very large heads, easy to persuade to produce an early crop – sow mid-spring and harvest midsummer.

'Rudolph'
Sprouting broccoli with bright purple spears, ready in time for Christmas if you are lucky.

'Shogun'
Calabrese with fine, domed heads.

'Trixie'
Very tender calabrese with lots of secondary spears that prolong cropping; good resistance to clubroot.

Perfect calabrese
Cover the crop with fleece for a really early harvest of succulent, gourmet florets.

These are a must for me because both my young son and I adore them lightly steamed or in stir-fries. The naming is confusing, but calabrese and broccoli are basically very similar. Sown in spring, calabrese is ready for eating in summer or autumn, whereas sprouting broccoli is overwintered and harvested the following spring. Both crops are also rather easier to grow than cauliflowers.

SITE AND SOIL Sunny, with an alkaline, free-draining but moisture-retentive soil.
SOWING OUTDOORS Early to late spring for calabrese, mid- to late spring for broccoli, in a well-prepared seedbed. Transplant from early to midsummer.
SOWING INDOORS Spring (*see p.23*), for planting out from early to midsummer.
FINAL PLANTING DISTANCE 30–45cm (12–18in) between plants, and 60cm (24in) between rows.
HARVESTING Late winter to autumn, with a range of varieties of the two crops.
APPROXIMATE YIELD About 750g (1½lb) per plant.

Keys to success

■ Sow in a seedbed (*see p.21*), then transplant seedlings to their final positions. Thin seedlings to at least 7.5cm (3in) apart within each row to encourage sturdy plants.
■ Transplant plants when 7.5cm (3in) tall and the soil is thoroughly moist.
■ Broccoli and calabrese need a regular supply of moisture to crop well. Mulch deeply on free-draining sites.
■ Cabbage root fly can be a problem (*see facing page*), and clubroot (*see p.35*) affects all brassicas including broccoli, calabrese and cauliflower. It is most damaging on heavy, acid soils, so liming (*see p.19*) and improving drainage helps to deter it. Always check bought-in plants and destroy any that have swellings on the roots. There is no reliable control, but if clubroot is a problem in your garden, raise plants in single pots that are at least 5cm (2in) in diameter. This allows them to develop well-established root systems before transplanting, so that they are better able to cope with clubroot attack.
■ Sprouting broccoli plants are often top-heavy when fully grown so may need staking if they are to stay upright.
■ Pigeons can be a real pest, especially in winter, so net crops and put up bird scarers if necessary.
■ It is time to harvest sprouting broccoli when the flowers are still in tight bud and the shoots are 15–20cm (6–8in) long. Pick regularly and each plant should crop for at least six weeks.

Cauliflowers

Although I'm not a great brassica fan (hence no cabbages in my garden), I do love cauliflower florets in a stir-fry or curry, or with a really rich cheese sauce. So I am attempting to grow a few cauliflowers, and I say "attempting" for the simple reason that they are notoriously difficult in my area. For a successful crop, they need to be entirely happy – with a deep, well-fertilized soil and never a hint of conditions that could cause a check in growth. But get it right, and the varieties available can, between them, provide crops from early spring through to early winter.

> "Cauliflowers transplant most successfully if watered well an hour or two before lifting, keeping plenty of soil in the rootball."

SITE AND SOIL A sheltered site in sun or partial shade and alkaline, moisture-retentive soil that has been well fed with compost or manure. Winter varieties need protection from frost.
SOWING OUTDOORS Varies with variety, so follow instructions on the seed packet. Sow in a seedbed (*see p.21*); transplant when plants have 5–6 leaves.
SOWING INDOORS Follow advice on seed packet. Harden off before planting out.
FINAL PLANTING DISTANCE 60–75cm (24–30in) apart, depending on variety.
HARVESTING Early spring to early winter, according to variety. Pick while the florets are tightly packed in the head.
APPROXIMATE YIELD One head of 500g–1kg (1lb 2oz–2lb 4oz) per plant.

Keys to success

■ Spring cauliflowers are in the ground for a long time and take up a lot of room. In smaller gardens, I recommend concentrating on early summer varieties, or those bred specifically for picking when young and small.
■ Purple varieties may lose their colour on cooking, but make an unusual and tasty addition to a plate of crudités.
■ Cabbage root fly is a common pest. Circles of old carpet, roofing felt, or proprietary discs fitted around the bases of plants work well (*see p.32*) if put in place immediately on transplanting. Alternatively, cover crops with fleece.
■ Anything that causes a check in growth, especially an inadequate or irregular water supply or extremes of temperature, is likely to result in undersized, often deformed heads. Regular watering and good soil preparation are essential, and it is also worth mulching the crop.
■ Cauliflowers, especially if they are to be overwintered, must not be given too much nitrogen (in manure, for example) or heads will be small and the plants less able to withstand low temperatures.
■ If exposed to severe winter weather, the heads may be damaged. To prevent this, fold the leaves over the curds, loosely tying them in if necessary. This will also help to protect summer varieties from being damaged by very strong sunlight.
■ Caterpillars can be a nuisance. If the plants are grown under horticultural fleece, well anchored at the edges, you should be able to prevent the butterfly from laying eggs and so keep the crop caterpillar-free.

Globe artichokes

Looking rather like a particularly large and elegant thistle, it is the flowerheads of the globe artichoke that make a delicious vegetable, especially when drenched in melted butter. These stately plants will reach 90–150cm (3–5ft) tall and, at their peak – from early summer until the end of autumn – are attractive enough to grace any herbaceous border.

SITE AND SOIL Lots of sun and a light soil that has had plenty of garden compost or well-rotted manure incorporated into it.

SOWING SEED Sow indoors in late winter to early spring, and outdoors in mid-spring. Harden off indoor-raised seedlings before planting out.

PLANTING Late spring, setting offsets 5cm (2in) deep and 1.2m (4ft) apart.

FINAL PLANTING DISTANCE About 1.2m (4ft) between plants.

HARVESTING Midsummer to early autumn.

APPROXIMATE YIELD Once established, about 10 heads per plant.

PIPPA'S SELECTION

'Green Globe'
Rounded heads of reliable quality; also readily available as seed.

'Purple Globe'
Very similar to 'Green Globe' but tinged with purple and the flavour not as good; particularly hardy.

'Gros Vert de Lâon'
Reliable and tasty; often sold as offsets.

Keys to success

■ Globe artichokes can be grown from seed, but I prefer to raise mine from offsets since seed-raised plants can be very variable in cropping and flavour. Buy offsets in spring or, even better, take them (also in spring) from a plant that you know performs well.

■ To take offsets, scrape away the soil from around the top of the plant and slide a knife down between each offset and the parent plant. Leave at least three shoots on the parent.

■ Young offsets need to be kept well watered and fed during their first year, while they are getting established.

> *"Be prepared to wait for your first crop and you will reap the rewards in subsequent seasons. "*

■ Although you might get one artichoke head in the first year, steel yourself and cut it off as soon as it forms. The plant will perform all the better in the following years.

■ Regular feeding and watering throughout summer are essential if the plant is to crop well.

■ Cutting the "king" bud – the topmost bud – encourages more heads to form. When harvesting, cut heads with short sections of stem attached.

■ Since artichokes are not always totally hardy, especially on heavy soil, in cold areas, or in particularly severe winters, insulate the crowns with a deep layer of straw. Remove it as the plant comes into growth in mid-spring.

Raise new plants
Planting rooted side shoots, or "offsets", is a good way of obtaining reliable varieties. Each offset needs only a small amount of root (*inset*). Trim away some of its foliage (*right*), and provide a little shade with fleece after planting, to help it establish easily.

Picking time Harvest just before the flowers open, when the scales are fleshy and still soft. ▷

Tomatoes

Whatever the labels claim, shop-bought tomatoes never have the flavour, juiciness, or texture of home-grown fruits so this is a crop worth finding space for, if at all possible. I am concentrating on outdoor varieties in my kitchen garden, but if you have room in a greenhouse for some indoor plants, then so much the better. Since flavour is a matter of personal taste, try growing one plant each of a range of types to find out what appeals to you most. The small tomato plants available at garden centres in late spring will save you raising lots of different varieties from seed.

SITE AND SOIL Outdoors, a sheltered spot with plenty of sun and good, fertile soil. In the greenhouse, indoor varieties do well in borders, pots, or growing bags.

SOWING INDOORS Sow seed at 65°F (19°C) in a greenhouse or on a sunny windowsill (*see p.22*). Sow greenhouse varieties late winter to early spring, and outdoor varieties late to mid-spring (try to time this for 6–8 weeks before the last frosts). Plant out only when plants have been thoroughly hardened off and all danger of frost is past.

FINAL PLANTING DISTANCE 45cm (18in) between outdoor plants (and in greenhouse borders), with 75cm (30in) between rows, or three plants to a growing bag.

HARVESTING Midsummer onwards for early-sown greenhouse varieties; late summer to early autumn or the first frosts for outdoor varieties.

APPROXIMATE YIELD Varies greatly with conditions and variety but about 1.75kg (4lb) per outdoor plant and 3.5kg (8lb) per indoor plant.

Keys to success

■ Prick out seedlings once they are large enough to handle easily (usually when at least three true leaves have formed) into individual 7.5cm (3in) pots of multipurpose compost (*see p.23*).

■ Harden off plants carefully before planting outdoors, or they will not be able to withstand the sudden change in conditions. Covering with fleece for the first week or so helps them to settle in.

■ Although growing instructions often refer to pinching out side shoots, this is not always necessary. On "indeterminate" varieties (which are grown as cordons), you need to remove the side shoots (*see below*) to produce a single-stemmed plant. It will need tying in to a sturdy cane, or similar support. "Determinate" varieties are grown as bushes and need little, if any, pinching out or support. Seed catalogues should state the type of tomato and whether pinching or staking is necessary. Most greenhouse varieties

Side shoot removal
Pinch out the side shoots between leaves and main stem on cordon types when 1–2cm (½in) long. Take care not to damage foliage or stem.

Ripe for picking
The long trusses on 'Gardener's Delight' provide fruit over a long period. For the best flavour, let tomatoes ripen fully on the plant.

are indeterminate, so must be pinched out, whereas many outdoor varieties are determinate bush tomatoes.

■ You will also need to "stop" tomato plants that are grown as cordons. When 4–5 trusses of fruit have formed, remove the growing tip 2–3 leaves above the topmost truss.

■ You can get a fair crop using a large container or growing bag in a sheltered, sunny spot. Keeping plants adequately watered can be extremely difficult, especially in really hot weather, so the larger the container the better. Make sure any pot you use is at least 25cm (10in) in diameter.

■ Tomatoes in containers are prone to blossom end rot (*see p.35*), a disorder caused by lack of calcium. Regular watering should prevent this occurring. Cherry tomatoes rarely succumb, whatever you do to them.

■ Feeding with organic soluble potash fertilizer will improve yields, especially on container plants. Alternatively, you could add rock potash to the soil prior to planting outdoor tomatoes. Liquid comfrey fertilizer also encourages good fruit formation.

■ Tough-skinned tomatoes are a real disappointment. Excessive heat and inadequate or erratic watering are usually to blame.

■ For a good crop outdoors, it really helps to have a sheltered site and a long, hot summer. To prolong the season, cover plants with fleece (or put cloches over small-growing varieties) as soon as temperatures start to drop at the end of summer.

■ In warm, muggy summers, outdoor tomatoes may succumb to tomato blight, the fungal disease that also often affects potatoes (*see p.35*). Spraying plants with a copper-based fungicide (acceptable to most organic gardeners) should help to prevent this, provided that you strike early enough. It is unusual for crops in greenhouses to be affected.

■ Greenhouse pests, especially whitefly, love tomato plants. I use a biological control – a tiny parasitic wasp called *Encarsia formosa*. This can be preceded by a tiny brown beetle, *Delphastus*, if the problem has got out of hand. Growing French marigolds or other highly aromatic plants among the tomatoes may also help.

■ Never risk growing tomatoes on the same piece of land more than once in every three years and always use new growing bags or fresh compost in containers. Tomatoes are prone to foot- and root-rotting diseases, which often build up in soil or re-used compost.

"Thinning foliage helps sunlight to reach fruit and ripen it, but don't get carried away or the plant will not be able to feed itself properly."

Old-fashioned charm
For tomato connoisseurs – and those who like a challenge – many of the heritage varieties, such as 'Green Zebra', combine excellent flavour with a distinctive appearance.

Sweet & hot peppers

For a really good crop of peppers, you do need a greenhouse or conservatory (although I once saw a thriving plant in a sunny porch). It is possible, however, to get reasonable results with some of the smaller varieties in a container in a sheltered, sunny spot, for instance the corner of a patio. I'm growing sweet peppers not only because I love their crunchy texture and tangy taste, but they look attractive, too. Chilli peppers, their hotter cousins, also make pretty plants, and strings of dried chillies look marvellous garlanding the kitchen.

SITE AND SOIL A greenhouse or very sheltered site outdoors. Peppers prefer slightly acid, fertile, well-drained yet moisture-retentive soil. In containers, use multipurpose compost.

SOWING INDOORS Early to mid-spring at 21°C (70°F). Plant out into the final growing position (in a container or greenhouse border) as soon as the first flowers develop. If plants are to go outside, harden them off carefully and wait until frosts are over.

FINAL PLANTING DISTANCE Two plants per growing bag or, if in a greenhouse border or open ground, about 40cm (16in) apart.

HARVESTING Midsummer to early autumn.

APPROXIMATE YIELD 6–8 sweet peppers or 20 chillies per plant.

Changing colours
If harvested green, sweet peppers take about three weeks to turn red. Some varieties mature to orange, purple, or yellow.

Keys to success

■ I have found that the collections of small hot pepper plants offered by some seed companies are a good idea. These allow you to grow a range of chillies with varying degrees of heat without having to buy and raise lots of different seeds.

■ Choose F1 hybrid varieties for growing outdoors in the British climate.

■ I prefer to sow seed in cells as this makes transplanting easier and saves time pricking out. If you grow them in trays, prick out seedlings when they have three or four true leaves.

■ Peppers do well in growing bags. If using containers, put one plant into a pot at least 25cm (10in) wide and deep.

■ Plants need quite a lot of care and resent conditions that don't suit them. Try to keep temperatures fairly constant and, if growing them in open ground, never plant into cold or wet soil. If in doubt, wait for better conditions.

■ Sweet pepper fruits can be heavy, and unless the plant is sturdy it may break under the weight of a good crop. Pinch out the growing tip of the main shoot (or shoots) when the plant is just over 30cm (12in) tall to encourage a sturdy stem structure.

■ Sweet peppers may succumb to blossom end rot, most commonly associated with tomatoes (*see p.35*). Regular but never excessive watering, combined with a moisture-retaining mulch, will help to keep plants growing strong and healthy.

■ Whitefly, red spider mite, and aphids (*see pp.32–34*) may also be a problem. Regular misting with water helps to deter red spider mite and also encourages fruit set.

Bright and beautiful Hot peppers justify their place in the garden purely as ornamental plants. ▷

Aubergines

Handle with care
Stems can be quite prickly and tough, so take care when picking aubergines. Always cut the fruits from the plant using a sharp knife; never try to twist or break them off the stems.

With their rich purple, unbelievably glossy skins, aubergines always remind me of the well-polished leather in a much-loved vintage motor car. Despite their almost too perfect appearance, they are versatile, succulent vegetables and, although you will get a better crop in a greenhouse, they will adapt well to life in a pot, provided you have a fairly warm and sheltered garden, backyard, or balcony. Not the most prolific of vegetables – and prone to a number of problems – aubergines are, however, one of the most rewarding crops to grow.

SITE AND SOIL Best in a greenhouse but will do well in a sheltered spot outside. A fertile soil or compost is essential.
SOWING INDOORS Early to mid-spring. Sow at about 21°C (70°F), then maintain a temperature of about 18°C (64°F) until planting time. Plant out into a greenhouse border or container when

the first flowerbuds appear. Plant outside or position outdoor containers only when frosts are over.
FINAL PLANTING DISTANCE Space plants 60cm (24in) apart if grown in open ground, under a cloche, or in a greenhouse border. You can fit three plants into a growing bag.
HARVESTING Midsummer onwards.
APPROXIMATE YIELD Hugely variable, usually 4–6 large aubergines per plant, but more if small.

Keys to success

■ I find aubergines in growing bags crop best if sited in a sunny, sheltered spot, preferably against a south- or west-facing wall. A deep pot – at least 25cm (10in) in diameter – filled with multipurpose compost, usually works even better because it gives plants plenty of room for their roots.
■ When all but dwarf-variety plants reach 30–40cm (12–16in) tall, pinch out the growing tips.
■ Keep plants well watered, especially those in containers, and feed regularly with an organic soluble potash fertilizer.
■ If you grow a heavy-cropping, large-fruited variety under perfect conditions, the plant may become overburdened. Be prepared to remove some young aubergines or support the laden stems.
■ Aubergines are prone to red spider mite and whitefly (see pp.33–34), especially in a greenhouse or frame or under a cloche. Regular misting with water helps to deter red spider mite, but biological controls may be needed.
■ In cooking, sliced aubergines are often sprinkled with salt then rinsed with water to remove the bitter taste, but I have never found this necessary.

Cucumbers

Since I can hardly imagine a salad without cucumber, I'm growing some outdoor types, but a greenhouse or large cold frame extends the range of varieties you can grow. The smooth-skinned fruits produced under glass will be better than their rough-skinned outdoor cousins, with fewer seeds to spoil your cucumber sandwiches.

> *"Cucumbers can suffer on transplanting so, if possible, raise outdoor varieties from direct-sown seed."*

SITE AND SOIL Very sheltered, sunny spot with fertile, well-drained soil for outdoor types. Incorporate plenty of organic matter if the soil is light.

SOWING OUTDOORS Sow outdoor varieties in late spring or very early summer, 1–2cm (½–¾in) deep. Protect with a cloche or upturned jam jars.

SOWING INDOORS Sow outdoor cucumbers from mid- to late spring, and greenhouse varieties mid-spring, at 21–24°C (70–75°F), in a propagator or heated greenhouse. Plant out when frosts have finished, after thoroughly hardening off.

FINAL PLANTING DISTANCE 60–75cm (24–30in) apart in an outdoor bed or greenhouse border. Put one plant in a growing bag or container.

HARVESTING Summer.

APPROXIMATE YIELD 10–12 fruits per plant in a slightly heated greenhouse (and more with more heat). Outdoor plants will produce fewer cucumbers.

Keys to success

■ When sowing outside, sow three seeds per station. Thin to leave the most vigorous seedling and water well.

■ Protect outdoor cucumbers from extremes of temperature and also from wind. Cloches or fleece are useful in the early stages. Give growing bags or pots the shelter of a wall or fence.

■ If growing a cucumber in a pot, the pot must be at least 30cm (12in) in diameter and 25cm (10in) deep. Choose a variety such as 'Bush Champion', and pinch out the growing tips when the plant has about seven leaves.

■ You will need to rotate cucumbers with other crops or change the soil in a greenhouse border every year or in alternate years. Plants are extremely susceptible to foot- and root-rotting infections that build up in the soil.

■ Train indoor cucumbers up string, netting, or canes, secured at top and bottom. Some outdoor varieties need support, but bush types do not.

■ Do not remove the male flowers (those that grow directly from stems, without fruits swelling at the bases) on outdoor cucumbers. On greenhouse varieties, however, any male flowers must be removed or the fruits may taste bitter. "All-female" varieties largely make this process redundant, but even they may produce a few male flowers if stressed!

■ Feed with an organic soluble potash fertilizer when the fruits start to set.

■ Under glass, whitefly and red spider mite are serious pests. Use biological controls (*see pp.33–34*) before numbers start to build up. Keep the air as humid as possible to encourage plant growth and keep red spider mite at bay.

Water conservation
Plenty of water is vital if plants are to crop well. A deep mulch around the plants helps to conserve moisture in the soil.

PIPPA'S SELECTION

'Burpless Tasty Green' Crisp, tasty, outdoor variety; thin-skinned, so should produce fewer adverse side-effects for those who suffer after eating cucumbers.

'Bush Champion' Good for containers; resistant to cucumber mosaic virus.

'Gracius' Seedless outdoor variety; short fruits, only 20cm (8in) or so long.

'Telegraph Improved' Reliable, dark green, greenhouse variety.

'Tyria' All-female greenhouse variety; long, seedless fruits that have a good flavour.

Courgettes & marrows

Provided that you give courgettes the conditions they need, they are one of the easiest vegetables to grow, ready to turn into tasty meals only a few months from sowing the seed. I love cooking them in casseroles and in stir-fries, or using them raw in salads. Choose the round types, or let your courgettes grow into marrows, and you can enjoy them filled with a delicious cheese, herb, and tomato stuffing.

SITE AND SOIL A sunny sheltered spot with well-drained, yet well-watered soil. Incorporate plenty of organic matter, such as well-rotted manure, into the soil to help conserve moisture.

SOWING OUTDOORS Late spring and early summer, setting two seeds where intended to grow, then thinning out the less vigorous seedling.

SOWING INDOORS Throughout spring, in 5–7.5cm (2–3in) pots (*see below*). Harden off; plant out after the last frosts.

FINAL PLANTING DISTANCE 60–90cm (24–36in) between plants.

HARVESTING Midsummer to early autumn.

APPROXIMATE YIELD 15 courgettes or five marrows per plant.

Keys to success

■ Whatever the catalogues and seed packets claim, I find that traditional green-skinned courgettes have a much thinner, more tender skin than golden varieties so I now grow only green types.

■ Plants can be badly affected by cucumber mosaic virus (*see p.35*), but there are plenty of disease-resistant varieties from which to choose.

■ Sowing in succession over a period of weeks seems to have little effect on the cropping time so does not help to avoid the inevitable glut.

> **"Remember that courgettes are prolific, so don't be tempted to plant too many."**

■ If you do not have a greenhouse, you can speed up the results of outdoor sowings by placing a small cloche, upturned jam jar, or the bottom section of a clear plastic drinks bottle over the newly sown seed.

■ Regular watering is essential. Drench the soil thoroughly, but avoid wetting flowers, foliage, or developing fruits.

■ Courgette and marrow flowers often rot off, especially in damp weather or if watered from overhead. Left unchecked, the developing crop can be spoiled, so remove deteriorating flowers promptly.

■ In cold seasons, or for early crops, try imitating bees by hand-pollinating the crop. Remove a male flower (which has no swelling at the base) and gently push its central parts into the centre of a female flower (which has a swelling at the base, like a miniature courgette).

Sowing seed
The large, flattened seeds are best sown on their sides, pointed end downwards. Push them into the compost or soil so that they are 2.5cm (1in) deep.

Perfect crop Courgettes are ready to harvest when about 10cm (4in) long. ▷

ROOT & STEM VEGETABLES

Carrots

Having trained in crop protection, I am all too well aware of the horrible chemicals that are often used to produce carrots commercially. By growing my own, I know that they will not only taste sweet and tender, but also that they will not be laden with organophosphates and other nasties. The only problem is that my fairly heavy soil is unlikely to encourage them to thrive, so I am concentrating on the shorter, or stump-rooted, types.

SITE AND SOIL Carrots prefer light, free-draining, fertile soil.
SOWING OUTDOORS Make successional sowings, about every two weeks, from mid-spring to midsummer. Sow seed 1cm (½in) deep in rows 30cm (12in) apart. For early crops, sow from very early spring under cloches.
FINAL PLANTING DISTANCE Thin seedlings to 7.5–10cm (3–4in) apart.
HARVESTING From late spring to early winter.
APPROXIMATE YIELD Hugely variable depending on variety, but about 500g (1lb 2oz) per 30cm (12in) row for maincrop carrots, slightly less for earlies.

Short and sweet
Stump-rooted carrots such as these are ideal for heavy, shallow, or stony soils. They may be small, but they will be packed with juicy flavour.

Keys to success

■ Well-prepared, deeply dug soil is essential. Avoid compacting the ground (by treading on it, especially while damp, for instance) or roots will be short or fanged (forked). Recently manured soil, or using too fresh manure, also increases the chances of fanging and other root deformities.

"Try intercropping rows of carrots with onions to reduce the risk of carrot fly. The smell helps to mask that of the carrots."

■ If you are short of space and do not mind smaller carrots, space rows 15cm (6in) apart.
■ Germination is very poor if soil is too wet or cold, and hopeless below 7°C (45°F), so only sow seed if conditions are right or under cloches.
■ Carrot fly is a potential menace because the larvae tunnel into roots, spoiling them and opening them up to rot. Covering the area with fleece should stop the fly laying eggs close to the crop. Alternatively, since the flies are low-flying, surrounding the crop with a 45cm (18in) high, fine mesh "fence" should also prevent the fly from damaging the carrots.

Swedes

- Sow seed sparsely to minimize the need for thinning. Crushed foliage helps the carrot fly to find carrots by smell. Be sure to remove any thinnings from the area. It is easier to sow the fine seed sparsely if you mix the seed with some silver sand first.
- Successional sowings of a range of varieties, early and maincrop, greatly extends the season.
- Regular watering should prevent roots from cracking or splitting.
- On light soil, carrots can stay in the ground well into winter. Lift them from heavy clay and store in boxes of sand.

Previously, I used to eat swedes for reasons of economy rather than because I enjoyed them. Now, not only I, but the whole family, like their flavour. At the tender age of five months, my son Callum grinned broadly when fed mashed swede and still seems to have retained a taste for the stuff. If you have never given swedes a go before, why not try them now.

SITE AND SOIL Sheltered, sunny site with fairly moisture-retentive, but well-drained neutral to alkaline soil.
SOWING OUTDOORS Early spring to early summer, about 2.5cm (1in) deep, in rows about 40cm (16in) apart.
FINAL PLANTING DISTANCE Thin seedlings to about 20cm (8in) apart.
HARVESTING Autumn to midwinter.
APPROXIMATE YIELD Roots may weigh up to 1kg (2lb 4oz) each.

Keys to success

- Thin the seedlings in stages, starting as soon as the first true leaves appear. Waiting any longer may prevent the roots on the remaining seedlings from developing as well as they should.
- Regular watering, especially in dry weather, is essential or the roots are likely to be small and woody and the plants liable to run to seed.
- Swedes, like other brassicas, are prone to clubroot (*see p.35*). Improving the drainage and liming the soil will help to reduce the problem.
- Flea beetles may make numerous small holes in the leaves, stunting the growth of seedlings. Covering young plants with fleece should prevent this.

> *"Swedes are one of the easiest of the root vegetables to grow."*

Root of the matter
For slim, tapered carrots, you need deeply dug, fine-textured soil. If roots encounter stones or unyielding clay, they may become fanged.

PIPPA'S SELECTION

'Best of All'
Sweet, mild flavour; easy to produce good, round roots.

'Marian'
Resistant to clubroot.

'Ruby'
Resistant to clubroot.

Parsnips

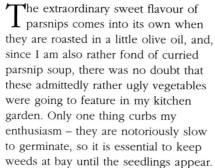

PIPPA'S SELECTION

'Avonresister'
Small, conical roots; good in stony or very heavy soil; the most resistant to parsnip canker.

'Cobham Improved Marrow'
Long roots; good resistance to canker.

'Tender and True'
Long roots with particularly good flavour.

The extraordinary sweet flavour of parsnips comes into its own when they are roasted in a little olive oil, and, since I am also rather fond of curried parsnip soup, there was no doubt that these admittedly rather ugly vegetables were going to feature in my kitchen garden. Only one thing curbs my enthusiasm – they are notoriously slow to germinate, so it is essential to keep weeds at bay until the seedlings appear.

SITE AND SOIL For long roots, you need a deep, neutral to alkaline soil with a fairly fine texture and no stones, in sun or slight shade. On less suitable soil, choose shorter rooted varieties. Canker disease is more likely on acid soil.

SOWING OUTDOORS Sow (*see below*) from mid- to late spring at regularly spaced intervals (stations), where you intend the parsnips to grow. Sow each clutch of seeds 10–15cm (4–6in) apart, in rows about 30cm (12in) apart.

HARVESTING Mid-autumn to late winter. Harvest as the foliage starts to die back.

APPROXIMATE YIELD About 500g (1lb 2oz) per 30cm (12in) of row.

Space saving
If you station-sow parsnips, you can sow a few lettuce or radishes in between. These germinate quickly and mark out the rows, making weeding easier. Both intersown crops will be ready to harvest before the parsnips develop and need all the space.

Keys to success

- The soil needs to be really well prepared, weeded, and raked and all sizeable stones removed. Keep it weeded while the seeds germinate.
- Parsnips often get canker; it is worth choosing disease-resistant varieties.
- Station-sowing – setting 2–4 seeds at regular intervals, or stations, along the row – is essential because germination is poor as well as slow. Simply weed out all but the most vigorous seedling if several appear at any one station.
- Birds may steal the seeds of any direct-sown vegetable but, because parsnips are so slow, the risk is all the

Wait for the flavour
You can start to harvest in mid-autumn, but roots will be all the sweeter after they are frosted.

Jerusalem artichokes

Roasting in olive oil gives these a delicious flavour, but I also like them boiled or made into soup. They grow so fast, they are perfect for "instant" gardening, although you have to wait until winter to harvest them. Expect the plants to reach at least 3m (10ft). They create a lot of shade, so be careful where you place them, but you can turn their height to your advantage and use them as a temporary shield against excessive sun or wind.

SITE AND SOIL Jerusalem artichokes seem to grow almost anywhere – in sun, shade, even in heavy soil.
PLANTING Plant tubers as soon as you buy them, usually early to mid-spring, setting them 30–40cm (12–16in) apart and about 10cm (4in) deep.
HARVESTING Winter.
APPROXIMATE YIELD About 2kg (4½lb) per plant.

Keys to success

■ You can make a few large tubers go further by cutting them into several pieces. If each section has a healthy-looking bud, it should form a plant.
■ Jerusalem artichokes can become invasive because any chunk of tuber left in the soil can grow into a new plant. To overcome the problem, plant tubers in a galvanized chicken-wire "basket" and simply lift out the basket when harvesting. Otherwise, take care to lift every piece from the ground.
■ In very windy sites, plants may get wind-blown, which reduces the yield. Earthing-up helps counteract this or, in extreme conditions, you can stake plants.

"In dry weather, artichokes can become even knobblier than usual; an occasional watering is worthwhile."

greater. Use bird scarers or protect the rows with taut lengths of cotton tied between sticks (*see p.21*).
■ Germination is poorest if the soil is cold and wet, so wait until conditions improve rather than risk sowing too early. Cover the ground with cloches or mini-polytunnels, if necessary (*see p.24*).
■ Small-rooted 'Avonresister' is useful if space is limited; sow at 7.5cm (3in) intervals in rows 15cm (6in) apart.
■ Water in dry weather or roots may split due to erratic moisture levels.

PIPPA'S SELECTION

'Fuseau'
Smooth-skinned, less knobbly tubers that are easier to prepare in the kitchen as well as less wasteful.

Potatoes

One of my earliest gardening memories is of "helping" my mother to lift potatoes. It was always an exciting moment as I rushed to gather the crop, and I still get that same tingle all these years later. Even if space is tight, I try to squeeze in a few tubers; they taste wonderful and I can be sure that they have been nowhere near unpleasant insecticides, a great comfort when eating them in their jackets or as new potatoes, lightly scraped, drenched in melted butter and chives. To avoid problems with slugs and wireworms (*see pp.33–34*) in my garden, I have concentrated on early varieties because these can usually be lifted before much damage is done. Maincrop varieties tend to be more severely affected.

Seed potato preparation

Chit seed potatoes, to make them shoot, by standing them "rose" end uppermost (the blunt end of the tuber with the most potential sprouts) in an old cardboard egg box or seed tray. Choose a cool, but frost-free, spot with plenty of natural light – I use a kitchen windowsill, but a cool spare room would be even better.

How to plant

Plant potatoes with the sprouted ends uppermost in a trench. Set tubers 7.5–13cm (3–5in) deep – the smaller the tuber, the shallower the depth.

SITE AND SOIL A sunny site with well-drained soil, preferably deep and fertile.
PLANTING Plant early varieties from early to mid-spring and maincrop varieties from mid- to late spring. Chit seed potatoes (*see left*) about six weeks before you intend to plant them; the sprouts should be 1–2cm (½–¾in) long at planting. Set tubers 7.5–13cm (3–5in) deep, depending on their size.
FINAL PLANTING DISTANCE About 30cm (12in) apart for earlies, with 40–50cm (16–20in) between rows, and 38cm (15in) apart for maincrop varieties, with 75cm (30in) between rows.
HARVESTING Early summer to autumn.
APPROXIMATE YIELD Varies hugely with variety and conditions, but usually 1–2kg (2lb 4oz–4lb 10oz) per plant for earlies, and 3–4kg (6lb 12oz–9lb 4oz) maincrop.

Keys to success

■ Always buy seed potatoes that are certified virus-free from a reputable supplier. It may be tempting to use potatoes that have sprouted in your vegetable basket, but these may not be virus-free and the long shoots will break easily when planted.

> "Potatoes, especially maincrop varieties, are a good crop on new land as their root systems help to break up the soil."

■ Avoid growing potatoes on very alkaline soils or on soil that you have limed recently since lime encourages scab disease. Also avoid any areas limed the previous season for growing brassicas. If scab is a problem, choose 'King Edward', 'Maris Peer', or 'Arran Pilot', which all have good resistance.
■ You can grow potatoes in any well-drained container that is at least 30cm (12in) deep and wide. Half-fill it with multipurpose compost, put in two tubers, and top up with more compost. Keep well watered.
■ To get an extra-early crop, I like to plant a favourite early variety, 'Concorde', as soon as the soil has dried out a little. I then cover the rows with low polytunnels to enable the soil to retain the warmth from sunny days and to protect young shoots from frost. Fleece works well, too.
■ As soon as shoots appear above ground, earth-up the rows. Do this regularly until there is a ridge 15cm (6in)

high along the row. Initially, this helps to protect shoots from frost; later it prevents tubers from turning green (green potatoes are poisonous and fit only for the compost heap). Earthing-up also helps to keep weeds down.
■ Potatoes are very prone to blight, which can seriously damage the crop, especially its storage potential. Many organic gardeners are happy to use copper-based sprays as soon as the muggy conditions that encourage the disease develop. I prefer trying to grow resistant varieties, such as 'Cara', 'Estima', 'Romano', and 'Maris Peer'.
■ In dry weather, you will need to water potatoes to get a good crop. An irregular supply can cause tubers to split or crack.
■ If potato blight does strike, I remove and destroy the damaged haulms (stems) at once, in an attempt to stop the spores spreading into the soil or on to the tubers. The resulting crop is then usually perfectly usable.

When to lift the crop
Lift early potatoes as soon as they are ready, usually as the flowers open. Maincrop types can stay in the ground until early autumn. Make sure that tubers are dry before storing in a cool, dark, frost-free place.

Onions

For my garden, I have concentrated on raising onions from sets – small, immature bulbs that are readily obtainable from garden centres and seed catalogues. They make life a lot easier, especially if, like me, you lack time and space for indoor sowing. On heavy soil, they are also less prone to pests and diseases such as onion fly and mildew. However, if you do decide to grow onions from seed, you will find the range of varieties is greater.

SITE AND SOIL Plenty of sun and well-drained, neutral to alkaline soil that is fertile, but not freshly manured.
SOWING OUTDOORS Plant sets as soon as soil is dry enough in spring, setting them so that their tips just protrude above soil level.
FINAL PLANTING DISTANCE Space sets about 10cm (4in) apart (for medium-sized bulbs), in rows 25cm (10in) apart.
HARVESTING From late summer to early autumn.
APPROXIMATE YIELD One onion per set, size varying with variety and spacing (*see right*).

PIPPA'S SELECTION

'Ailsa Craig'
Large and mild-flavoured; does not store well.

'Autumn Gold'
Large bulbs; should keep until mid-spring following an autumn lifting; good resistance to bolting.

'Fen Globe'
Very resistant to bolting.

'Jagro'
Early cropping, from midsummer; resistant to bolting.

'Red Baron'
Red-skinned; early cropping.

Preparing for storage
Onions need to dry off before being stored if they are to keep well through the winter. Lay them out on dry ground or on some raised netting or wooden slats.

Keys to success

■ Onions will vary in size when mature, depending on how closely the sets or seedlings have been spaced. For large bulbs, space sets 15cm (6in) apart.
■ If you plant sets too shallowly, you may find that birds whip them out before they have had a chance to root. If birds do remove or loosen them, replant as soon as possible.
■ If you choose "heat-treated" sets, onions should not bolt (run to seed).
■ Regular weeding, done carefully so as to avoid damaging the bulbs, is essential if the onions are to develop properly. Their rather sparse, strappy foliage will do nothing to help smother competing weeds.
■ Onion neck rot, where the neck end deteriorates and the rot then spreads down into the bulb, can be a problem, especially if growing conditions have been poor and it has been damp at harvest time. Red-skinned varieties seem to be less vulnerable.
■ Onion fly (*see p.34*) can be a problem, but if you plant your onions (and leeks and garlic) close to your carrots all the crops should suffer less from pest damage.
■ You can lift and use onions fresh, but they will not be ready to store until the foliage starts to yellow and die back. Bending the leaves over the bulbs while they are still in the soil (often recommended) is not a good idea: it is likely to hinder good ripening of the bulbs and reduce their storage life.
■ Once you have lifted the bulbs, leave them outside in a well-ventilated,

Leeks

warm, but not too hot, place for one or two weeks so that they can dry off thoroughly before being stored. If the weather is dry, you can leave them on the soil surface; if it is wet, place them in a cool greenhouse or cold frame.

- Store onions (and garlic and shallots) in a dry, well-ventilated spot, out of direct sun, in net bags or shallow trays, or plait them into strings. Good air circulation hinders the spread of disease. Damp starts them into regrowth.

- Shallots are grown in much the same way as onions, usually from sets, except that you can plant them earlier, from midwinter to early spring, and they are also ready to harvest a little earlier. As each set develops, it forms a small cluster of bulbs, so give shallots a slightly wider spacing of 15cm (6in) between sets and 30cm (12in) between rows. Harvest as for onions.

GARLIC

Plant individual cloves 2.5–5cm (1–2in) deep and approximately 15cm (6in) apart. Well-drained soil and a sunny site are essential. As my soil is rather heavy, to improve the drainage I planted the cloves in ridges, each ridge about 10cm (4in) high. Use cloves bought from a garden centre or seed catalogue, not the supermarket, as these may harbour virus infections.

   Plant once the weather is suitable, generally in early to mid-spring (or in autumn if the soil is very well-drained) and lift the bulbs as the foliage starts to yellow, usually late summer.

Easy to grow and a useful winter vegetable, leeks are something I heartily recommend you try. They take up little room, but if you want to get two crops from the space of one, you could even grow a few small, fast-maturing lettuces in between the rows. The aroma from the leeks should also help to keep aphids away.

SITE AND SOIL Leeks are not too fussy about site and do well in most soils.
SOWING OUTDOORS Sow thinly in early to mid-spring, about 1cm (½in) deep, in rows 15cm (6in) apart, in a seedbed.
SOWING INDOORS Midwinter to spring, sowing seed thinly in trays, pots, or cells, planting out in early summer.
FINAL PLANTING DISTANCE 15cm (6in) between plants and rows.
HARVESTING Late autumn to mid-spring.
APPROXIMATE YIELD Plants may weigh 110–180g (4–6oz) each.

Keys to success

- If you want early crops, sow the seed under glass in mid- to late winter.
- Plant out or transplant seedlings when they are about 20cm (8in) tall. Make individual holes for each, about 15cm (6in) deep, using a dibber. If the foliage is very long, trim it slightly before planting. Water well; this provides moisture and also washes soil into close contact with the roots.
- If you get your early potatoes planted and harvested promptly, you can plant leeks on the same site.
- Leeks thrive on plenty of food, but giving them too much nitrogen (for instance, in the form of animal manure) makes attacks by rust (*see p.35*) more likely because the foliage is so soft.

(*see p.35*)

PIPPA'S SELECTION

'Alvito'
Late-maturing; rust- and bolt-resistant.

'Conora'
Late variety; rust- and bolt-resistant.

'Neptune'
Late variety; resistant to rust.

'Autumn Mammoth 2 – Walton Mammoth'
Early maturing; good resistance to rust.

Planting pattern
If leeks are planted into deep, individual, pre-formed holes, it allows the stems to expand easily while being blanched at the same time.

CULINARY HERBS

Choosing & growing

There is no better way to enhance or complement the flavours of home-grown vegetables than with some freshly picked herbs. Annuals are worth raising from seed, sown every few weeks to obtain a continuous supply of leaves (*see growing details overleaf*). Most perennials, however, are best bought as plants, particularly those with ornamental foliage or flowers. Give the shrubby types a pot of their own or, in mixed containers, keep them in check with regular pruning.

The right site

Herbs are not difficult to grow, but if they are to produce plenty of tasty growth over as long a timespan as possible, the majority need ample sun and a really well-drained soil. In heavy or damp conditions, most will look unhappy and be extremely short-lived. Because of this, I decided to grow my herbs in containers rather than in the open ground. Containers have many advantages: they look attractive, you can position them wherever you want, and you can use the growing medium that best suits the plants instead of having to rely on your garden soil.

When deciding where to grow your herbs, choose a spot where you will be able to get to them easily and to enjoy them, as well as one that suits the needs of the plants. Having to trudge out to a vegetable plot a long way from the house every time you need a few sprigs to add to your supper is a real

disincentive, especially on a dark, rainy evening. Containers can also be moved to a more sheltered spot if the weather suddenly turns very wet or cold, often allowing you to pick your herbs over a much longer period than if they were growing in a bed or border.

Better drainage

If you do opt to plant herbs in the open ground, you must make sure that the site is really well drained. Adding organic matter and large quantities of grit helps to improve drainage, and is necessary on all but the lightest soil. When growing herbs in pots, I use a multipurpose compost, sometimes mixed with a loam-based compost, into which I incorporate about 20–30 per cent grit. A deep layer of crocks at the bottom helps to ensure that drainage holes are kept clear. Terracotta suits herbs particularly well, but provided the drainage is good you can use any type of container that appeals to you and fits with your style of garden.

Most herbs can be grown in a pot, but always check the plant label and make sure that the chosen container is sufficiently large, especially if you are planning a mixed planting. I prefer to put large shrubs, such as bay and rosemary, into their own individual pots. Mint, too, is best planted on its own or it soon engulfs its companions. For a mixed container, my favourite herbs are chives, sage, marjoram, and the thymes. All are perennial and both

Texture and taste
Non-invasive herbs combine well in one large container. Here, chives, marjoram, sage, and thyme supply a variety of foliage and flavour.

sage and thyme are evergreen so they will keep their leaves through most winters. I also like to add in a few annual herbs and find that basil, in particular, works well.

Decorative leaves

If you think of herbs as dull-looking plants with foliage only in unremitting shades of green, think again. Many (including thyme and chives) have superbly pretty flowers or silver, purple, or brightly variegated leaves. Textures vary, too – think of spiky chives and rosemary, crinkly curled parsley, and the felted surface of sage.

You can raise herbs from seed but, if you need just a few plants and want to be able to enjoy the fantastic array of leaf colours and flavours, it is worth buying small, sturdy pot plants from a good specialist nursery or garden centre. It will work out cheaper in the long run. Also, since named varieties,

including those with the most attractive foliage or flowers, cannot usually be raised from seed, buying plants will give you the best and widest choice.

Herbs on ice

During the height of the season, plants will probably produce more growth than you can possibly eat. To keep them growing well, however, and producing fresh, tender leaves, most herbs benefit from regular harvesting. Take advantage of this and make some herb ice-cubes to perk up meals in the leaner months of the year.

As those grey-green, nearly tasteless offerings in the supermarket illustrate, most herbs do not dry well (except for rosemary and bay). Instead, chop up individual portions of your favourites and put them into ice-cube trays. Top up with water and freeze straight away. When you need some leaves out of season, pop a cube or two into the cooking and the result is as close to fresh herbs as you can get.

"Herbs are decorative, so grow them in a spot where you can enjoy them."

Individual containers
Large plants, such as bay, rosemary, and santolina, will be happiest in their own pots, but they can be grouped with smaller pots of parsley and thyme.

CINNAMON
BASIL

CHIVES

CORIANDER

POT MARJORAM

Basil

I adore basil, whether chopped into a salad, pounded into pesto, or flavouring an Italian supper. It is an annual herb, and as its popularity has increased, so has the number of varieties available as seed. I had great fun with my exotic selection of basils. Cinnamon and lemon basils have a distinct aroma, and Thai basil, ideal for stir-fries, is spicy, with attractive red-tinted leaves. If you want a particularly small plant, then 'Minette', at 15cm (6in) tall, is perfect. The compact varieties look great in containers and perform better than other types in a pot on a windowsill. For a gorgeous, dark purple leaf, try 'Red Rubin' or 'Purple Delight'. Basil can even be used as a path edging.

Basil is tender, so sow the seed indoors from late winter to late spring, shallowly, at 21–24°C (70–75°F). When seedlings are large enough to handle, prick out into individual 7.5cm (3in) pots. You can keep the plants growing on a windowsill or, once frosts have finished and after hardening off, plant them out into well-drained soil in plenty of sun or into a herb container.

Bay

Bay can grow into a 6m (20ft) tree, so this is a herb that needs its own sizeable pot or space in the garden, although it can be kept within bounds by regular trimming. Give it a sunny, sheltered spot and good drainage. For the first couple of years after planting, it is a good idea to provide some winter protection. You can wrap pots in hessian or bubble-wrap; in very cold winters or in cold areas, move pots into a sheltered spot or greenhouse for winter. A golden-leaved form is available, but it is more easily damaged by frost and wind than ordinary bay.

Chives

The dark green, spiky foliage and the purple pompon flowers borne in early summer make chives the perfect candidate for edging beds. They also look marvellous in a container. They are perennial, but the leaves die down in winter. White-flowered garlic or Chinese chives, with a distinct taste of garlic, are also well worth growing.

Sow seed 1cm (½in) deep from mid- to late spring direct into a well-prepared seedbed. Thin to about 15cm (6in) between plants. Seed can also be sown in cells of multipurpose compost in a propagator at 19°C (66°F). Sow about 15 seeds in each 2.5cm (1in) cell, and transplant as a clump once frosts are over. Alternatively, buy a pot of chive plants. Within a year or two the clump will be large enough to divide.

Coriander

This is another annual herb I cannot resist, although it is hard to grow well because it runs to seed so easily. The tangy, almost citrus-like flavour of the foliage makes it useful in cooking – in curries, in sauces, and in salads. It is happiest grown in the ground (on a windowsill it quickly becomes drawn and leggy). The strain 'Cilantro' seems to perform best of all.

A sheltered, well-drained site in full sun is essential. Sow seed thinly from mid-spring, raking the soil just over the seed, then thin out seedlings as soon as they are large enough to handle. To ensure a constant supply of foliage, sow seed every two weeks or so.

Marjoram & oregano

I prefer to buy plants although some marjorams and oreganos can be raised from seed. The range includes annuals and perennials. Sow direct into a prepared seedbed in spring, or into individual cells, at a temperature of 15°C (59°F). Leave the seed uncovered on the surface. Do not be disappointed if germination is poor. A well-drained soil and plenty of sun are essential, but you can grow the golden-leaved forms in a shady position since they often scorch in full sun. The pretty purple flowerheads will attract bees.

Mint

Definitely best bought as a plant. The wide range of mints includes varieties with undertones of apple, spearmint, ginger, or lemon in their flavour. Choose a site with fairly moist soil in sun or shade. Mint can be invasive, so prevent it from spreading in open ground by planting it in a large bucket with the base cut off. Generally, the variegated forms are less thuggish, but you will still need to stay on the alert. Plants soon increase in size and need to be divided every two years or so. Keep cutting shoots throughout summer to encourage plenty of tender new leaves. Mint is perennial, but its foliage disappears in winter.

Parsley

Both curled and flat-leaved varieties are attractive as well as useful, and are best grown as annuals. Parsley likes well-drained soil in sun or partial shade. Sow the seed thinly in drills 20–25cm (8–10in) apart, from early spring to early summer. Thin out in stages so that plants are eventually 20cm (8in) apart. Alternatively, sow seed in cells in a heated propagator at 18°C (64°F). This produces an earlier crop because germination is speedier and seedlings can be planted out as soon as the weather warms up. Cutting back hard

and watering well encourages fresh crops of leaves. Covering plants with cloches in autumn allows you to harvest parsley for as long as possible.

Rosemary

The needle-like foliage and grey-blue flowers make this a pretty evergreen shrub. Buy plants and give them a large container or well-drained site that has plenty of sun. Plants have a tendency to sprawl; cut back immediately after flowering to help keep the growth compact. To propagate, take cuttings in spring or summer and root them in very well-drained compost.

Sage

A shrubby, evergreen perennial available in many different-coloured leaf forms. 'Tricolor' has green and white foliage with a distinct pink flush when young (but beware, this is not as hardy as other sages), and 'Icterina' has bright green and yellow-variegated leaves. Sage needs a very well-drained, sunny site. Buy plants; named varieties do not come true from seed. Take cuttings as for rosemary (*see above*).

Thyme

The huge range of varieties gives you a choice in foliage colours and textures, and sometimes flavour as well. Try a lemon-scented variety, for example. Thyme needs well-drained soil or potting compost and plenty of sun, particularly for the most pungent aroma. The pretty pink, purple, or white flowers attract bees. Trimming back plants after flowering helps to keep them compact. Plants can be shrubby or can form spreading mats. To propagate, take softwood cuttings in spring, or divide creeping types.

OREGANO

PLAIN-LEAVED PARSLEY

ROSEMARY

PURPLE-LEAVED SAGE

TREE & SOFT

FRUIT

Most fruit is easy to grow. If you do not have room for it among your vegetables, it deserves a place elsewhere in the garden, for it is highly ornamental. Tree fruit can be trained against walls and fences and strawberries planted in pots. In these pages, the soft fruits, such as raspberries, follow the apples, plums, and pears.

Apples

There is something about an organically grown apple, picked and eaten straight from the tree, that is hard to beat. The crunch as you bite into it, followed by the juiciness and the flavour, are fantastic and the knowledge that it is free from pesticides only adds to the enjoyment. When choosing which varieties to grow, you will need to consider the taste, texture, and season of the fruit, the rootstock on which the tree is grown, and the pollination group to which the variety belongs, because you need trees that can pollinate each other if you are to get a good harvest.

SITE AND SOIL A sunny site with well-drained, yet moisture-retentive, soil.
PLANTING Plant bare-root trees while dormant – not in leaf – between late autumn and early spring (*see facing page*). Container-grown trees can be

planted at any time provided that the soil is not frozen or waterlogged but, like bare-root trees, they are easiest to look after and settle in if planted in late autumn. Spacing between trees depends on rootstock, size, and shape of tree, so check the details on the label.

HARVESTING Summer until early autumn, depending on variety.

Keys to success

■ The rootstock onto which a tree has been grafted affects its eventual size and to some extent the conditions it will need. For apples, there are several different rootstocks available, ranging from the extremely dwarfing M27 to the vigorous M111. The following three are likely to be the most useful.

■ M9 is very dwarfing. It produces a bush tree 1.8–3m (6–10ft) tall and is also good for cordons, but it needs permanent staking and a lot of maintenance, including watering.

■ M26 is semi-dwarfing. It produces a bush tree 2.5–4m (8–12ft) tall and is also good for cordons and espaliers with two or three tiers. It does well in most conditions and should be ready to start producing fruit in three to four years. The apple bushes I have chosen are all on M26 rootstocks.

■ MM106 produces a large bush tree, 3.6–5.5m (11½–18ft) tall. It is good for other shapes, too, and is suitable for less favourable sites, including those with light, free-draining soils.

■ If space is limited or if your garden has some bare expanses of fence or wall, you can grow cordons – single-

Thin heavy crops
In midsummer, trees naturally shed some of their fruits. Afterwards, if a tree is still heavily laden (*see inset*), you may need to thin some more. Remove sufficient apples – especially any that are small or malformed – to give the remainder room to develop and ripen.

stemmed trees trained at an oblique angle – or espaliers (*see p.13*). Cordons give you the chance to fit in several varieties, improving pollination.

■ Trees must be in blossom at the same time if they are to cross-pollinate. Catalogues from fruit nurseries will give flowering times or pollination groups. Often a tree in a neighbouring garden will do the trick.

■ When planting, never allow the roots of bare-rooted trees to dry out. Dig the hole before unwrapping them. If they seem at all dry, soak them in a bucket of water for a couple of hours first. Prune out any damaged roots.

> "Take time and care over planting, so that you give your tree the best possible start."

■ Make sure there is ample room for the roots when digging the planting hole – it usually needs to be at least 60cm (2ft) across. Check the depth of the hole by standing the tree in it. When it is planted, the graft point (the swollen joint near the base of the stem) should be just above the soil surface.

■ Use a short stake (pressure-treated with preservative) to support the tree, driving it securely into the hole before planting. Position the stake so that it is just off-centre. Use a tree tie with a spacer, and check it regularly so that, as the trunk grows, the tie never becomes too tight or chafes the bark.

■ Water thoroughly after planting and remember that regular drenchings are essential if the tree is to establish well.

■ Fruit trees need to be pruned immediately after planting (*see p.31*).
■ If there is a very heavy crop, you will need to thin fruit (*see facing page*).
■ Trees may be affected by apple and pear canker. Roughened, loose areas of bark appear on branches, occasionally ringing the branch and causing dieback. Prune out completely and destroy the affected wood. Try to improve growing conditions, especially drainage, since wet soil may aggravate the disease.

Good planting
Dig an ample hole and fork in plenty of organic matter. Check the depth and spread out the roots. As you back-fill, jiggle the tree up and down to settle soil between the roots. Gently firm with your foot (*see inset*) and water in well.

Plums

Although plums can be tricky to grow, largely because the blossom comes early and is more likely to be damaged by frost, there are more plum than apple varieties that are able to set fruit without a second tree to act as a pollinator. My kitchen garden is by no means small, but even so, fruit trees need space and so it made sense to ensure that the one plum I allowed myself was self-compatible – able to fertilize itself. I opted for 'Victoria'. It is especially reliable and the fruits can be used for dessert or cooking.

SITE AND SOIL Sunny position, with a moisture-retentive, but not over-wet, soil. Protection from cold winds early in the year is essential.

PLANTING Plant bare-root trees between late autumn and early spring, while they are dormant. They can be heeled in temporarily if the ground is frozen or waterlogged. Container-grown trees can be planted at any time of year, but they are easiest to look after and more likely to establish well if they are planted in late autumn. The spacing depends on rootstock and tree shape; check the site has sufficient room before buying.

HARVESTING Late summer and early autumn, depending on variety.

Keys to success

■ The two rootstocks usually on offer are the dwarfing Pixy, which needs very fertile soil and life-long staking, and St Julien A, which is semi-vigorous and produces trees up to 6m (20ft) tall.

■ In cooler areas, or where space is at a premium, train plums as cordons or as a fan against a suitably warm fence or wall. Growing Minarettes, which naturally develop into upright, single-stemmed trees that need little pruning, is another way of saving space.

■ Plant carefully, digging a good-sized hole and incorporating plenty of well-rotted manure or garden compost (*see previous page*). Plant to the correct depth so that the graft point (the swollen joint near the base of the stem) is just above soil level. When staking trees, ensure that the buffer-spacer on the tree tie is in the correct place – between tree and stake – so that there is no risk of the bark being damaged. Loosen it periodically as the tree grows and the trunk expands.

■ Frosts killing blossom can be a regular problem, even in a relatively sheltered site. If at all possible, protect the tree with some horticultural fleece on particularly cold nights.

Long live Victoria
'Victoria' is one of the most useful varieties. The fruits are juicy, and the blossom is self-fertile as well as being good at pollinating other plums. It is also one of the best varieties for growing in cooler parts of the country.

■ Netting trees against birds (which may strip trees of leaf- and flowerbuds) is sometimes necessary in some areas.

> *"Prune plums only in summer, while trees are growing well, to avoid the risk of silver leaf."*

■ Like apples (*see previous page*), trees naturally shed some fruits in midsummer. If necessary, remove more, so that the remainder are 5–10cm (2–4in) apart.
■ Plums (like other stone fruits such as peaches, nectarines, cherries, gages,

and damsons) are prone to silver leaf, a potentially fatal disease. Trees develop a silvery sheen on the foliage on isolated branches and affected limbs then die back. A central brown stain is clearly visible if the wood of branches over 2.5cm (1in) in diameter is cut across. Prune back affected branches well past the stained area. To reduce the risk of infection, prune only during the summer months and paint all wounds over 1cm (½in) in diameter with a wound treatment. Bin or burn the affected wood.
■ Because of the danger of silver leaf disease, prune only when absolutely necessary and then do it in summer while the tree is growing well.

Sweet temptation
Plums look especially tempting, hanging from the tree in late summer, but they also attract wasps. If these become troublesome, you could try making a trap for them by half-filling a jam jar with beer (*see p.32*).

Pears

PIPPA'S SELECTION

'Beurré Hardy'
Good-sized fruits in early autumn; juicy and often described as having a flavour of rose-water.

'Concorde'
Produces heavy yields of fine-flavoured fruits; stores well.

'Conference'
Good pollinator and partially self-fertile; fruits store well; does better than most in cool areas.

'Doyenné du Comice'
Mid-autumn fruits; very juicy and gorgeous flavour.

'Williams' Bon Chrétien'
Very juicy and sweet; reliable, but not heavy-cropping; sadly vulnerable to scab disease.

Grow your own pears and you can savour their melt-in-the-mouth texture and juicy sweetness to the full. You can also enjoy the fruits properly ripened and not bruised, as they often are when you buy them. It is worth remembering that if they are to crop well, pears need more warmth than apples, largely because they flower before apples and so are more likely to be damaged by spring frosts.

SITE AND SOIL Choose a sheltered, warm position. Pears grow well in all but very sandy or very heavy soils. On light or even slightly shallow soils, they will require regular watering as well as generous layers of mulch.

PLANTING Plant bare-root trees as soon as soil conditions are suitable and the plants are available, usually from mid-autumn to early spring. Container-grown pears can be planted at any time, but if you avoid summer planting it will make after-care easier.

Time to pick
Pick pears when still firm, before they are fully ripe. Lift the fruit slightly and twist. If it parts easily from the tree, it is ready to pick.

HARVESTING Mid- to late summer through until early autumn, depending on the variety.

Keys to success

■ Pears are usually grown on quince rootstocks: there is a choice of just two. Quince A suits most tree shapes and soil types. Quince C can be used for cordons, but for other shapes it needs a very fertile soil.

■ To get a decent crop, you will need a couple of pear trees in reasonable proximity so that their blossom will be pollinated. Check pollination groups when buying and make sure that flowering times overlap.

■ Dwarf pyramids, espaliers, and cordons, are the best shapes for small gardens or restricted spaces.

> "In cool areas, choose cordons or espaliers, and give them the protection of a wall."

■ Plant bare-rooted trees from autumn to early spring (see p. 79). Prune them immediately after planting (see p. 31). Planting container-grown trees at this time also means that they will be kept well-watered in the early stages and so given the best possible start.

■ In the same way as apples, pear fruits thin themselves naturally in midsummer, but once this has occurred, it is best to thin fruit again to leave one or two pears per cluster.

■ Trees occasionally suffer from canker, which can be treated (see p. 79).

Blackberries & hybrid berries

My love of blackberries is such that, although I live where there are lots of brambles in the hedgerows, I still decided to squeeze a plant into my garden. They are a versatile fruit and if you add one of the hybrid berries, such as a tayberry or loganberry, you should be able to gather crops from summer until the first frosts. You can also enjoy the fruits out of season, since they freeze really well. Although blackberries have a deservedly bad reputation for their thorns, there are some thornless varieties, which make siting and looking after them very much easier.

SITE AND SOIL Plants prefer full sun and moisture-retentive but well-drained soil; they still crop fairly well in part shade. Avoid very exposed or cold sites.

PLANTING Plant about 5–7.5cm (2–3in) deep, spreading out roots well to encourage the suckers that will form the new canes. Plant bare-root canes in winter; container-grown plants can be

Tomorrow's feast
An abundant harvest need not go to waste. Blackberries can be enjoyed out of season since they freeze particularly well.

put in at any time of year but winter or early spring is preferable. The spacing between plants can vary from 1.8–5m (6–15ft) depending on variety, so check the label before you buy a plant.

HARVESTING Midsummer to autumn, depending on variety.

Keys to success

- Buy your plants from a reputable supplier and make sure that they are certified virus-free.
- Most blackberries need some sort of support over which they can scramble. Use a network of wires on a fence, wall, or framework of posts (like those for raspberries, *see overleaf*). A length of trellis also works well.
- Plants need plenty of well-rotted manure or garden compost added to the soil before planting if they are to grow vigorously and fruit well.
- After planting, prune each cane to about 20cm (8in) above soil level, cutting back to a vigorous bud. Like raspberries, newly planted blackberry canes and hybrid berries enjoy a deep mulch of well-rotted manure or garden compost to help conserve moisture in the soil and keep down weeds.
- As plants grow, tie the canes into the supporting wires or trellis.
- If water is in short supply, the most important time to apply it is just as the first berries start to colour up. This increases the ultimate size of the fruits.
- Potash encourages abundant crops. Apply rock potash according to the instructions on the packet.
- In late winter, prune out the canes that fruited earlier in the year. Train in the new canes, spacing them evenly across the supporting wires or trellis.

Raspberries

Remove old canes
With summer-fruiting varieties, at the end of the year, cut back the old canes which fruited during that year.

Eaten on their own or accompanied by some vanilla ice-cream, freshly picked home-grown raspberries are in a class of their own. I was so keen to get my chosen varieties into the ground that we put up the support system of poles and wires in the evening, after dark, so that we could film planting them the very next day. The only drawback at the start is that you have to wait a year for your first crop, unless of course you do as I did and include some autumn-fruiting types that will produce berries in their first season.

SITE AND SOIL Well-drained soil, preferably neutral to acid.
PLANTING Plant canes from late winter, once the soil has dried out sufficiently, until early spring. Set canes 45cm (18in) apart. If you grow more than one row, allow 1.8m (6ft) between rows.
HARVESTING Mid- to late summer, and late summer to mid-autumn for autumn-fruiting varieties.

Keys to success

■ The support system I am using consists of four pressure-treated timber posts, each 2.7m (9ft) long with about 45cm (18in) driven into the ground and set 4m (12ft) apart. Three horizontal galvanized wires, 75cm (30in), 1.2m (4ft) and 1.7m (5ft 6in) above ground level, are stretched taut between them. Because the site is rather windy, the posts are strutted for extra support.
■ If you want raspberries but cannot face putting up posts and wires, try 'Autumn Bliss', which can be grown without support.
■ Where space is at a premium, you can train raspberries up a single post – a pressure-treated post driven firmly into the soil so that about 1.8m (6ft) remains above ground. Plant two or three canes around the post and, as the canes develop, loop them and tie them into the post with twine.

"If soil is waterlogged or frozen at planting time, heel in plants until the weather improves."

■ Should the roots of the canes be at all dry, soak them in water for a couple of hours before planting.
■ Plant the canes quite shallowly, about 5cm (2in) deep, and spread the roots horizontally in the planting hole or trench to encourage the formation of suckers. It is the suckers which later develop into the new canes.

■ Immediately after planting, cut each cane back to a healthy-looking bud 23–30cm (9–12in) above soil level. When the new shoots appear, cut off the old canes.

■ Mulch canes after planting to conserve moisture in the soil, and every spring in subsequent years.

■ As the new canes develop, tie them in to the wires. Allow about seven canes per plant, removing any surplus in late spring or very early summer. Dig or pull the canes out rather than cutting them off to avoid regrowth.

■ Good weed control is essential. A deep mulch helps to suppress weeds but hoe regularly if necessary, taking care not to damage emerging canes or roots close to the surface.

■ At the end of each year, on summer-fruiting varieties, cut out the woody, brown canes that bore fruit during the summer. Remove surplus canes in spring, limiting the number, as before, to about seven per plant and cutting out any that show signs of disease or are too far from the row. With autumn-fruiting varieties, cut all the canes to ground level. Berries will be produced on the canes that shoot up in spring.

■ Unless they succumb to virus or other diseases, raspberry canes should continue to crop well and will need replacing only every ten or so years.

Incomparable flavour
Raspberries produce the most luscious fruits when they have plenty of moisture. Prepare the ground well and dig in lots of organic matter, such as well-rotted manure, before planting. For trouble-free crops, buy only canes that are certified virus-free.

Strawberries

Whether you plant them in the kitchen garden or flower borders, or are restricted to growing them in containers, you should certainly find space for some strawberries – although you are more than likely to find that squirrels, slugs, snails, or birds take their fair share, too. Strawberries are almost impossible to store, so choose a selection of varieties that will fruit over as long a period as possible, then use cloches or some other sort of protection (*see p.24*) to extend the cropping period even further.

SITE AND SOIL Strawberries tolerate most kinds of soil, but do best if it is slightly acid and fairly moisture-retentive, but not heavy. If the soil is too wet, diseases such as crown rots and grey mould are likely. On chalky or alkaline ground, leaves may yellow between the veins, due to iron and manganese deficiency. If these soils cannot be avoided, treat affected plants with sequestered iron.

PLANTING Runners (small rooted plantlets) are best planted in autumn. However, I put in mine in late winter and they have established well, despite the cold, miserable weather to which they were subjected initially. Small pot-grown plants are usually available in spring and early summer and should be planted as soon as possible.

FINAL PLANTING DISTANCE 30–45cm (12–18in) between plants and 75–90cm between rows.

HARVESTING Early summer until mid-autumn, if you have a good selection of varieties and can give plants some protection, for instance with cloches.

APPROXIMATE YIELD About 750g (1½lb) of fruit per plant, once established.

Keys to success

- Always obtain runners or plants from a reputable source and buy those that are certified free from virus infection.
- The best and heaviest crop is usually produced in the plants' second year. They should crop well for four years or more, unless viruses or other serious infections strike.
- When planting runners, make sure that the roots are spread out and that the base of the crown is just below soil level. Planting too shallowly or too deeply may cause the plants to crop poorly. Firm in new plants really well.
- Strawberry pots make ornamental planters and can hold a range of varieties. you can also use growing bags, which are less decorative but very productive, although these provide a temporary planting only and are rarely productive after the second year.

Remove runners
Pinch out runners (the strawberry's natural way of propagating itself) as soon as they develop, to encourage the plant to keep producing fruit.

A clean crop

A layer of straw under the ripening fruit helps to keep strawberries clean, but watch out for the slugs and snails it may also harbour.

"Grow a range of strawberry varieties for a summer-long crop."

■ Adding rock potash to the soil, according to the instructions on the packet, helps to encourage a good crop. If, in the first year, plants do not seem to have established well, remove some or all of the flower trusses to allow all available energy to be used in improving plant growth.

■ If grey mould is or has been a problem, make sure that all possible sources (usually dead and dying foliage on the strawberries or other plants) are removed. Also try to improve air circulation by giving plants plenty of space. If any fruits show signs of infection, remove them immediately, before the spores spread.

■ Any plants that become stunted and yellowed are probably infected with viruses and should be burned or binned immediately, before the problem spreads.

ALPINE STRAWBERRIES

If you want to grow alpine strawberries for that delicate, almost perfumed flavour, plants are easy to raise from seed. If you sow early enough, they will fruit in their first year. They produce their tiny berries from midsummer to late autumn, and grow better in cooler conditions than most strawberries. 'Alexandria' and 'Mignonette' varieties are sweet and juicy.

Sow seed from midwinter to early spring at about 21°C (70°F) and prick out the seedlings when they have two true leaves. By early summer, plants should be large enough to put in the garden.

Melons

Preventing rot
A ripening melon may start to rot if it rests on damp soil. Tuck a slate, tile, or small piece of wood underneath to protect it.

These are not the easiest of fruits to grow in the garden but, even without a greenhouse, it is possible to achieve some success although you need to choose varieties carefully. The crop may be small, and the sprawling plants certainly need space, but the feeling of pride when you offer guests some of your first honey-sweet melon is second to none.

SITE AND SOIL Preferably a cold greenhouse or large cold frame, but some varieties will crop outside in a sheltered spot. Rich, well-manured soil is essential.

SOWING INDOORS Late winter to mid-spring at 15–20°C (59–68°F), about 1cm (½in) deep, in individual cells or small pots. If growing under glass, transplant to the permanent position when seedlings have about four true leaves. If planting outside, pot on the seedlings, then harden off and plant out once frosts have finished or provide adequate protection (*see p.24*).

FINAL PLANTING DISTANCE About 90cm (3ft) apart.
HARVESTING Late summer.
APPROXIMATE YIELD Maximum four fruits per plant.

Keys to success

- If growing in a greenhouse border, cold frame, or open ground, plant on a slight mound after incorporating plenty of well-rotted manure.
- You can grow melons in growing bags, but they need to be well fed.

> *"Melons are thirsty and need regular and plentiful watering wherever you grow them."*

- Once the side stems have produced about five leaves, pinch out the growing tip of each. The shoots that develop from each side stem must then be pinched out again once they have produced three leaves.
- Pollination may be erratic. It helps if you take a male flower and push it into the centre of the female flowers (which, like those on a courgette, have a slight, but distinct, swelling at the base).
- The fruits will need support if the melon plant is trained up canes or wires. "Hammocks" made from old pairs of tights work well. If plants are allowed to scramble, protect the fruits from damp soil (*see left*).
- Once the fruits start to ripen, keep them dry and, if under glass, ensure that air circulation is good.

Rhubarb

One of the best ways of obtaining a good-flavoured plant is to sample the rhubarb grown by friends or family, then persuade them to let you have a section of the crown. Crowns are also readily available from seed catalogues, specialist nurseries, and potted on (at a greater price) from garden centres. I wouldn't recommend growing plants from seed. Once established, rhubarb is an easy, handsome-looking crop.

SITE AND SOIL Grows on most soils, but best results come from slightly acidic, fairly heavy, but not waterlogged, ground. Choose an open, sunny site and manure well before planting.
PLANTING From late autumn to early spring, as soon as crowns are available and while plants are dormant.

Keep it in the dark
Forcing rhubarb will give you an early crop. I use a traditional terracotta forcer, but an upturned black plastic bucket works just as well.

FINAL PLANTING DISTANCE Space plants 90cm (3ft) apart.
HARVESTING Late spring into summer, but can be forced for an earlier crop.
APPROXIMATE YIELD Depends on variety and age of plant.

Keys to success

■ Sections of the crown, or "sets", must have at least one bud and some fibrous roots; they are usually about 10cm (4in) across. Divide only plants that are healthy and vigorous; those growing poorly are often infected with viruses.
■ Rhubarb is a hungry, thirsty crop, needing plenty of food and water. After planting, never let crowns dry out or they may die.
■ Mulching, to keep the soil moist during spring and summer, encourages a large crop. A mulch of well-rotted manure or garden compost will also feed plants and is best applied in autumn or spring.
■ If you want to force your rhubarb, cover the crowns in early or midwinter with dry straw or leaves, then cover with a terracotta forcer or bucket (*see left*).
■ Do not harvest stalks until the second year. Never be tempted to taste the leaves as they are highly poisonous.
■ Occasionally rhubarb produces flowering stems. Cut these back as soon as they appear because, as they die back, they encourage crown rots to develop which can kill the plant.
■ Divide established clumps every three years or so.

"Pull off stalks rather than cutting them to reduce the risk of rot developing in the crown."

SOWING & HARVESTING CALENDAR

THE TIME AT WHICH CROPS can be sown and harvested varies from area to area and year to year, according to the weather. In frost-free parts of the south-west, sowing outside can usually start a few weeks earlier than in the north. It is not worth sowing tender crops indoors too soon in the season unless you have a suitable place to keep the young plants growing well until frosts are over. Nor should seed be sown outside into soil that is very wet or cold. This chart (*continued overleaf*) gives a general guide to sowing and harvesting times. For more specific details, turn to the page given by the crop name.

CROP	WINTER			SPRING			SUMMER			AUTUMN			SPECIAL REQUIREMENTS
	EARLY	MID	LATE	EARLY	MID	LATE	EARLY	MID	LATE	EARLY	MID	LATE	
AUBERGINES p.58				•	•			■	■	■			Tender; sow inside; the earliest crops are produced when grown under glass.
BASIL p.74			•	•	•	•	■	■	■	■			Raise early plants on a sunny windowsill; later outdoor crops need a sheltered site.
BEANS, DWARF FRENCH p.47				•	•	•	• ■	■	■				Sow inside for planting out after frosts, or sow later, in situ, direct into the soil.
BEANS, CLIMBING FRENCH & RUNNER p.46					•	•	• ■	■	■				As dwarf beans, above.
BROCCOLI, SPROUTING p.50			■	• ■	• ■	■							Sow in a seedbed and transplant later to the final growing position.
CALABRESE p.50					•	•	•	■	■	■	■	■	Sow inside for the earliest crops; a range of varieties will extend the season.
CARROTS p.62		■			•	• ■	• ■	• ■	• ■	■	■	■	Make successional sowings of a range of varieties for the longest harvesting period.
CAULIFLOWERS, SUMMER & AUTUMN p.51					•	•		■	■	■	■	■	Choose mini, summer, and autumn types. Sow in a seedbed for transplanting later.
CHILLI PEPPERS p.56					•	•		■	■	■			Tender; sow inside and grow under glass or in a sunny, sheltered site.

● = *Sowing*   ■ = *Harvesting*

WINTER: Early = *December*, Mid = *January*, Late = *February*   SPRING: Early = *March*, Mid = *April*, Late = *May*
SUMMER: Early = *June*, Mid = *July*, Late = *August*   AUTUMN: Early = *September*, Mid = *October*, Late = *November*

CROP	WINTER			SPRING			SUMMER			AUTUMN			SPECIAL REQUIREMENTS
	EARLY	MID	LATE	EARLY	MID	LATE	EARLY	MID	LATE	EARLY	MID	LATE	
CHARD p.38					●	●	●	■	■	■	■	■	Sow in situ. White-stemmed varieties usually crop for longer than red-stemmed types.
CHIVES p.74					●	●	■	■	■	■	■		Sow inside or outside.
CORIANDER p.74					●	● ■	●	● ■	■	■	■		Runs to seed quickly. Sow small amounts frequently, in situ, for a good supply of leaves.
COURGETTES & MARROWS p.60				●	●	●	●	■	■	■			Sow inside for planting out after frosts, or later direct into the soil and protect with a mini-cloche.
CUCUMBERS p.59					●	●	●	■	■	■			Make earliest sowings indoors; choose greenhouse or outdoor varieties as appropriate.
GARLIC p.71				●	●				■		●		Plant cloves direct outside; the more free-draining the soil, the earlier you can plant.
JERUSALEM ARTICHOKES p.65	■	■	■	●	●								Tubers planted in spring will produce a crop the following winter.
LEEKS p.71	■	● ■	● ■	● ■	● ■							■	Sow inside from winter to spring and plant out in early summer; or sow outside in spring.
LETTUCE pp.40–42	● ■	● ■	■	●	● ■	● ■	● ■	● ■	■	● ■	●	● ■	Winter varieties can be grown under cloches or in a cold frame to give a year-round harvest.
MELONS p.88				●	●	●			■				Usually grown under glass but there are one or two varieties that will succeed outdoors.
ONIONS (FROM SETS) p.70				●				■	■				Plant sets direct, in situ; foliage must be dried off thoroughly before harvesting and storing.
PARSLEY p.75				●	●	● ■	● ■	■	■	■			Grows well from an outside sowing but germination is slow.

● = *Sowing* ■ = *Harvesting*

WINTER: Early = *December*, Mid = *January*, Late = *February* SPRING: Early = *March*, Mid = *April*, Late = *May*
SUMMER: Early = *June*, Mid = *July*, Late = *August* AUTUMN: Early = *September*, Mid = *October*, Late = *November*

CROP	WINTER Early	WINTER Mid	WINTER Late	SPRING Early	SPRING Mid	SPRING Late	SUMMER Early	SUMMER Mid	SUMMER Late	AUTUMN Early	AUTUMN Mid	AUTUMN Late	SPECIAL REQUIREMENTS
PARSNIPS p.64					●	●							Sow direct in situ; the seed is slow to germinate; harvest as needed through winter.
	■	■	■								■	■	
PEAS p.44		●	●	●	●	●	●						Sow round-seeded types for the earliest crops, and wrinkle-seeded varieties for a summer harvest.
						■	■	■	■				
PEPPERS, SWEET & HOT p.56				●	●								Tender; raise seed inside and grow under glass or in a very sheltered spot.
								■	■	■			
POTATOES p.68				●	●	●							Choose between early and maincrop varieties and plant accordingly.
							■	■	■	■			
RADDICHIO p.43					●	●	●	●	●				Hardy; can be harvested outside in winter. A range of varieties gives a long season.
	■	■	■	■			■	■	■	■	■	■	
ROCKET p.43					●	●	●	●	●	●	●		Grows very fast. Sow a little often for a continuous supply. Cover autumn crops with cloches.
	■					■	■	■	■	■	■	■	
SHALLOTS p.71		●	●	●									Plant bulbs in winter once the ground is workable. Harvest as for onions.
									■				
SPINACH p.38					●	●	●			●	●		Sow direct in situ, using summer and winter varieties as appropriate.
	■	■	■			■	■	■	■	■	■		
SPINACH, BEET OR PERPETUAL p.38					●	●	●	●	●	●			Sow direct; a summer sowing can be harvested through winter.
	■	■	■	■			■	■	■	■	■		
SWEDES p.63				●	●	●	●						Sow direct in situ; harvest as required from autumn to winter.
	■	■								■	■	■	
SWEET CORN p.48					●	●	●						Tender; make early sowings inside. Protect direct-sown seed outside with mini-cloches.
								■	■	■	■		
TOMATOES, GREENHOUSE & OUTDOOR p.54			●	●	●								Sow greenhouse types from late winter; sow outdoor varieties inside to plant out after frosts.
								■	■	■	■		

● = *Sowing*   ■ = *Harvesting*

WINTER: Early = *December*, Mid = *January*, Late = *February*   SPRING: Early = *March*, Mid = *April*, Late = *May*

SUMMER: Early = *June*, Mid = *July*, Late = *August*   AUTUMN: Early = *September*, Mid = *October*, Late = *November*

USEFUL ADDRESSES

ADVICE & INFORMATION

Henry Doubleday Research Association
Ryton Organic Gardens
Ryton-on-Dunsmore
Coventry CV8 3LG
Tel: 01203 303517
http://www.hdra.org.uk
E-mail: enquiry@hdra.org.uk
HDRA has a 10-acre organic display garden at Ryton, another at Yalding, and a walled kitchen garden at Audley End. It runs events and workshops on subjects as diverse as pruning, potagers, and compost-making, organizes local groups, publishes factsheets and books, and runs a Heritage Seed Library. It also has an information-packed website and collaborates with Chase Organics in bringing out the Organic Gardening Catalogue (see Seed Suppliers).

Yalding Organic Gardens
Benover Road
Yalding
Near Maidstone
Kent ME18 6EX
Tel: 01622 814650

Audley End Organic Kitchen Garden
Audley End House
Saffron Walden
Essex CB11 4JG
Tel: 01799 520444

Brogdale Horticultural Trust
Brogdale Road
Faversham
Kent ME13 8XZ
Tel: 01795 535286
Home of the national fruit collection; organizes courses, demonstrations, fruit festivals, and tasting days.

SEED SUPPLIERS

As well as vegetable seeds, many seed companies also sell fruit plants.

D.T. Brown & Co Ltd
Station Road
Poulton-le-Fylde
Lancashire FY6 7HX
Tel: 01253 882371
Fax: 01253 890923

Mr Fothergill's Seeds
Gazeley Road
Kentford
Newmarket
Suffolk CB8 7QB
Tel: 01638 552512
Fax: 01638 750468

S.E. Marshall & Co Ltd
Wisbech
Cambridgeshire PE13 2RF
Tel: 01945 583407

The Organic Gardening Catalogue
Riverdene Business Park
Molesey Road
Hersham
Surrey KT12 4RG
Tel: 01932 253666
Fax: 01932 252707

Simpson's Seeds
27 Meadowbrook
Old Oxted
Surrey RH8 9LT
Tel & fax: 01883 715242
Tomato, pepper, and unusual vegetable seed specialists.

Suttons
Woodview Road
Paignton
Devon TQ4 7NG
Tel: 01803 696321
Fax: 01803 696345

Thompson & Morgan Ltd
Poplar Lane
Ipswich
Suffolk IP8 3BU
Tel: 01473 688821 (601090 for catalogue only)
Fax: 01473 680199

Edwin Tucker & Sons Ltd
Brewery Meadow
Stonepark
Ashburton
Newton Abbot
Devon TQ13 7DG
Tel: 01364 652403
Fax: 01364 654300
Good potato list.

Unwins Seeds Ltd
Histon
Cambridge CB4 9LE
Tel: 01945 588522
Fax: 01223 237437

BIOLOGICAL CONTROLS & SUNDRIES

Agralan
The Old Brickyard
Ashton Keynes
Swindon
Wiltshire SN6 6QR
Tel: 01285 860015
Fax: 01285 860056
Fleeces, barriers, etc; some biological controls.

Defenders Ltd
Occupation Road
Wye
Ashford
Kent TN25 5EN
Tel: 01233 813121
Range of biological controls, traps, and barriers.

English Woodlands Biocontrol
Hoyle Depot
Graffham
Petworth
Sussex GU28 0LR
Tel & fax: 01798 867574
Large range of biological controls.

The Organic Gardening Catalogue
Wide range of organic sundries and biological controls (for address, see Seed Suppliers).

INDEX

Page numbers in *italic* refer to illustrations.

ACKNOWLEDGMENTS

Author's acknowledgments

I would like to thank everyone who made this book possible, especially: the many staff at Dorling Kindersley, including David Lamb, Mary-Clare Jerram, and Lee Griffiths; special thanks to Pamela Brown for her unremitting help and great editorial skills; Dave King for the jacket photograph; and Peter Anderson for most of the photographs taken in the kitchen garden. Everyone at Catalyst Television, especially Colette Foster and Richard Thompson, plus all those involved in the filming of *Gardeners' World* for their enthusiasm. Richard Massey of Marshall's Seeds and Maggie at the HDRA for their valuable advice, plus the many companies who supplied seed, cloches, and so forth. Alasdair (and the boys) and Bill for helping so much, and Lisa for keeping an eye on those young seedlings (and my very precious young seedling) while I was working away from home.

The publisher would like to thank the following for their kind permission to reproduce their photographs:

(t = top, b = bottom, r = right, l = left, c = centre)

Garden Picture Library: Howard Rice 55br, 76–77, 80bc; Jacqui Hurst 88bl; Jerry Pavia 43tc; John Glover 55tl; Marie O'Hara 70b; Mayer/Le Scanff 49, 64–65, 69tr; Michael Howes 85t; Neil Holmes 83bl; Sunniva Harte 39; **Holt Studios International**: Gorden Roberts 46tr; Nigel Cattlin 58bc; Primrose Peacock 87tl; **Jacqui Hurst**: 24bl; **Nadia Mackenzie**: 5bl, 12tl, 53; **Clive Nichols**: 45r; **Photos Horticultural**: 5br, 12br, 41, 63bl, 71br, 81t, 82bc; **Howard Rice**: 61; **Tessa Traeger**: 89bl.

Illustration Gill Tomblin

Jacket photograph Dave King